One Step at a Time

*My 18-Month Walk
Across America*

ELENA J. HANUSE

Edited by Sandi Gelles-Cole

RAWSON ASSOCIATES : New York

To Bucky,
my gentle hero, who with unflagging loyalty
followed and often led me

Library of Congress Cataloging-in-Publication Data

Hanuse, Elena J.
  One step at a time.
  1. United States—Description and travel—1981–
2. Hanuse, Elena J.—Journeys—United States.
3. Walking—United States. I. Gelles-Cole, Sandi.
II. Title.
E169.04.H37   1987   917.3'04927 [b]   87-20664
ISBN 0-89256-321-4

Published simultaneously in Canada by Collier Macmillan Canada, Inc.
Produced by Rapid Transcript
Composition by Folio Graphics Co., Inc.
Designed by Jacques Chazaud
First Edition

Contents

Acknowledgments

A mighty thank you to the following: Eleanor Rawson, who believed in my story; Alice Babineau, an everlasting lifetime friend; Jeanne and Tom Gunn and Jean and Bill Dwyer, in whose homes this book was born; Alex, for believing in and sharing my dream; America; and my fellow Rotarians.

One Step
at a Time

ONE

··

Going
for a Dream

I left San Francisco on the fourth day of January in 1984 to start a 3,900-mile walk across continental America. I said when I left that I would be at the Statue of Liberty eighteen months later, on July 4, 1985. I was there, and I was there on time.

I knew when I began my walk that either Bucky, my floppy-eared Doberman, or I might not survive the journey. Yet there we were at its finish, Bucky at my heels, ready to go the last 2,370 steps of what I knew would be a 9,240,000-step trip. (Alex, my husband, had surprised me with that figure, arrived at by first determining how many steps I took in ten feet and then doing the necessary multiplication.)

We turned into Liberty State Park in New Jersey, which lies on the bank of the Hudson River, and followed Statue of Liberty Drive, passing the flags of the fifty states one by one. They lined the avenue as far as the eye could see and fluttered in gentle currents of air on that brilliant summer day.

My two sons had flown in from San Francisco to join us, and my heart was beating faster as we walked the last mile together. There she was, Miss Liberty herself, a soaring silhouette framed by the splendid New York City skyline. Mayor Anthony Cucci, of Jersey City, came out to walk the last steps with us, accompanied by a crowd of happy well-wishers who cheered us on. We got as close as possible to the Lady in the Harbor, separated only by the river, and that's when I broke down and cried.

I started my journey from the north end of the Golden Gate Bridge in San Francisco, a choice that was not random. In 1937, when I was only six years old, my mother took me to the opening-day ceremonies at the bridge. I clearly remember standing beside her, holding her hand, while she pointed westward over the rail and said, "Out there, Elena, lies the world." But even then I turned and faced the other way, looking out toward the thousands of miles of my country, and even then I dreamed of walking it.

For the next forty-six years, I nurtured my dream, storing it in that special place in my mind where I put those things that I'd like to do "someday," always letting the activities of life supersede those dreams. "One day," I would think, "I will see my country and its people in a way that will give me a true experience of it, walking coast to coast, from San Francisco to New York. One day I will do that, stopping to talk with as many fellow Americans as possible. I really will see America—smell it, taste it, and feel it."

"One day . . ." You know how good we are at setting dreams aside, keeping them only dimly alive for that elusive "one day." I didn't meet anyone along the road incapable of dreaming, or of having a personal collection of "somedays."

During all those forty-six years, I did exactly what so many people told me they were doing, and during that time, I, too, would have told a walking lady: "I've always dreamed about doing something like that. I'd like to see my country that way—just take off—but, you see, I don't have the time . . . I don't have the money . . . I'm too young . . . I'm too old . . . But someday I'd like to do that, too."

Just a few weeks after my husband, Alex, and I were married, in October 1980, I shared my dream with him for the first time: "Alex, do you know what I'd really like to do? I'd like to walk across America."

Alex didn't laugh, although three years later he would tell me he hadn't taken me seriously. During those years, I spoke of my dream perhaps three or four more times. And without saying a thing to me, Alex began to evaluate the depth of my seriousness. He began by testing my physical aptitude, as he had had experience in training for and participating in a variety of competitive sports. At the time, he understood the advantages of physical preparedness better than I. He was already familiar with my ability to make a mental commitment and keep it. But the idea of my walking across the continent when I could not even walk a mile down the neighborhood road—well, that tested his ability to believe that I could walk the country!

He started jogging with me around the block, easily running circles around me, and he encouraged me to walk greater and greater distances daily. My overall health was terrific, but I had absolutely no experience of physical activity to fall back on. I'd grown up in a San Francisco much more conservative than it is today, and my father had not approved of my participation in physical activities of any kind. It was simply not ladylike, in his opinion. I could read, embroider, study musical instruments, and of course help around the house, but the most athletic thing I'd ever done was to roller-skate in safe little loops on the hill in front of our home—and after several skinned knees I'd even given that up. I never even learned to dance.

So, with Alex supporting my aspirations, I succeeded eventually in walking one nonstop mile. That was a big deal! And

I persisted. Soon I could do two miles; and then five; then seven. After six months I had increased my mileage to an incredible (for me) nine nonstop miles!

Early in the fall of 1983 Alex and I drove through the vineyards over the rolling Sonoma hills to the Mendocino Coast. Out there, the cliff-hugging highway had more rolling elevations than the flat roads I had been walking. We were celebrating Alex's fifty-third birthday. As part of my gift to him, I had decided to surprise him by beating my existing record. That day I walked 15.5 nonstop miles. It was too much. The next day I could barely move. But the walking did serve to bring up the subject of my dream again. And that's when I realized how much quiet, strong support Alex had been giving me.

"You really want to do that, don't you?" said Alex.

"It has always been there for me."

"We could drive it."

"It's not the same; I'd be skimming the surface. I want to walk through the heart of America. The time has come."

"Then if you want to do it, do it, and I'll support your doing it."

So, suddenly, my dream was born. Like a bubble, it burst from that place in my mind where I store ideas in embryo. My dream had taken on a life of its own. Yes, I would do it. The only question for us now was *when*.

To my surprise, and to show me his total participation in my journey, Alex had already planned my route. "I've been looking over a map of the United States," he said, "and I have plotted a tentative itinerary. It's not a straight line, not even close to it, but it does take into consideration the continent's weather conditions. You can't walk the Rockies in winter, you know. You really need to be there in July or August, and if you walk, let's say, an average of eight or nine miles a day, it would take you six months just to be at the foot of those mountains. So you'd better leave early next year. It will be in the winter, but it will also give you some time to prepare."

We picked January 4, 1984. It would give me four more months to get ready physically and mentally, and we also decided we'd all go—Alex, Bucky, and I.

When I met Alex, I was divorced and seeing several other men. They were all nice people, but they were also very traditional, and I was unwilling to step into a marriage with conditions of dependency and control. After all, I had by then reared the two children from my first marriage, mostly by myself, and I had established myself in two careers, as both an educator and a real estate investor-developer. I didn't need a husband to provide me with either financial security or protection. Yet, in the depths of my heart, I held a need to share my life deeply. I was holding out, looking for a soul-mate, not really sure what that meant or that such a person even existed. But I knew I'd rather be lonely than settle for anything less than a relationship of loving support between two people who believed life should be an adventure of mutual and personal satisfaction.

Alex and I found that in each other. And while he was willing that I take my journey into America alone, when we saw a way of sharing the experience together, we jumped at it, because both of us can slip in and out of the roles of support or leadership. For us life is about supportive happiness and not domination.

We decided that Alex would plan my itinerary and be my support system, but—and this was important to me—never would he be on my heels. I wanted a truly deep personal experience of America. I wanted to see what couldn't be seen from rolling along in a car. I wanted to talk with people I wouldn't talk with if I stayed at home. And I wanted to handle whatever would come up between me and America.

On the road I'd be alone, though not entirely. We didn't ask him but we naturally assumed that Bucky, our one-and-a-half-year-old happy-go-lucky Doberman, would want to accompany me. It was amusing that many people thought I took him along to protect me, but that's a reputation Buck hasn't earned. The generality that all Dobermans are naturally vicious is just not true, and no one has ever taught Bucky to be mean. So Buck bears the brunt of a prejudice he doesn't deserve, although until you get to know the lovable nature of this playful, friendly dog, it can be unnerving, because our red-haired ninety-three-pound Dobie will demonstrate his affection whether you want him to or not.

Alex, as a computer expert, would take with him his IBM P.C. so he could continue working on the programs he was designing. We decided we would buy a recreational vehicle (or "R.V.," as some people call it) to house the computer. This vehicle ultimately became Alex's office as well as a place for all of us to sleep at night. It would be our home away from home for the eighteen months it was going to take me to walk across the continent.

I waited until December to tell my grown sons about my plan, partly because I was not completely convinced that I could make the January 4 departure date (there were so many details to iron out) and also because, at the bottom of my heart, I needed time to prepare for a last meeting—almost as if I might not ever see them again. I worked like crazy to finish a hooked rug, which I had worked on for three years, that I knew would be very special to Gary, my older son, and I gathered items that I knew Guy, my other son, would like to have. Although Alex and I told the two separately, they had almost the same reaction.

"Your mom and I are going on a trip," Alex began.

"Oh, that's nice. Where are you going?"

"Across the country, to New York."

They both responded with surprise. It was evidently a longer trip than they had anticipated.

"How long will you be gone?"

"Eighteen months."

"Eighteen months! Eighteen months?"

"Yes," explained Alex to each of my sons, "but," and here he paused, "your mom is doing it differently. She's going to walk it."

As well as my children know me and my adventurous spirit, they were nonetheless completely overwhelmed with surprise. And yet each in his own way recognized how right the trip was for me.

From Guy: "Mom, if anybody can do it, you can. Go for it!" And from Gary: "I know you'll find a way to make it, Mom."

Thus, the hardest part of preparing to leave was handled; the emancipation for all of us was complete. We would love each other as much as ever. I never felt that the geographical distance would separate us, because in spirit we were united. With their blessing, I was opening doors to another productive period of life.

Meanwhile, I was still walking my daily miles, in preparation for the journey. "It's important that you start training on more demanding roads," Alex told me. "Thirty-nine hundred miles in eighteen months is an average of eight miles a day. That may seem easy, but things will happen that may prevent you from walking even that far on some days. You want to visit schools, which will slow you down. There will also be days when you won't feel well. So you must be prepared to walk twelve, fifteen, twenty miles—even more on some days—and not just on flat roads."

"How about if I trained on Calistoga Road?" I chose that road because it was close to our home and because it has two demandingly steep hills on it.

"It would be perfect."

I began training in earnest at the end of a long sweltering summer. The temperatures still hovered in the nineties and on some days soared to a sizzling 107 degrees. The newspaper headlined it, people grumbled about it, and summer-tanned children shrieked through the spray of sprinklers on brilliant green lawns. Surrounding this placid country community, the

Sonoma County hills were already burned to a crisp. Earlier I had hiked over them when poppies were scattered in knee-high waves of grass; now even the insects had abandoned the sun-scorched earth. It was the languid end of summer when everything moved in slow motion except inside our sprawling ranch-style house. There a beehive of activity was going on.

Cardboard boxes crammed with books and records, pots and pans, were stacked and mounting ever higher against the walls. I yanked armfuls of clothing out of the closets and threw them on the bed, sorting them into piles. This jacket could go to Goodwill; this peach silk robe was to be stored—I couldn't imagine a need for it on the road. And this old blue shirt with holes in the sleeves that I'd saved for painting that I might do "one day" could now be thrown out.

Alex was emptying shelves in his office, throwing away computer catalogs he'd kept for years. The house was beginning to take on the appearance of denuded disorder. Wherever there was an empty surface, maps and more maps were spread. Poor Buck seemed at his wit's end, running from one end of the house to the other, lifting an ear in one direction then the other, trying to make sense of what was going on.

And every morning before the dew lifted from the lawn and before early commuters competed for the road, I'd jump out of bed with growing excitement, pull on my sneakers and sweats, and slip silently out the door.

I had chosen Calistoga Road because of its difficulty. This two-lane road winds 12.6 miles over the Sonoma County countryside, connecting Santa Rosa with the town of Calistoga. Calistoga is best known for its sparkling mineral water and steaming mud-bath spas. I held those nurturing treatments out to myself like a carrot on a string, promising to indulge in both when I made my first nonstop walk between the two communities.

The narrow asphalt road has two demanding hills. The first doesn't give an inch to a warm-up. It climbs immediately— 3.5 serpentine miles at a brutal 20 percent grade. After a brief but welcome plateau where the road widens and is bordered by pastures, the second hill climbs an exhausting 5.5 more miles, at a 16 percent grade.

Most highways are not graded in excess of 6 to 8 percent. I figured that these stiff slopes would serve as solid preparation for the valleys and peaks of the continent. I started out with a fledgling's unrealistic enthusiasm, expecting that my new pair of running shoes (the first of eighteen pairs) would carry me over the top of the first hill, which I named "Old 20 Percent." But I soon discovered my limitations. I couldn't walk even the smallest part of my training ground without stopping to catch my breath; and in no time at all I was dripping with perspiration. Using the back of my hand to wipe my chin, I set my jaw, renewed my determination, and shoved off again.

Soon I knew I shouldn't have worn my new red-hooded sweatshirt. I peeled it off, knotted the sleeves around my waist, rolled up my baggy sweatpants to just below my knees, and began again. My route was dismally discouraging. Nine miles on flatland roads was no preparation for this. I'd expected the hills to slow me down, not bring me to a halt. I was forced to take the grade even more gradually. I crisscrossed back and forth, resenting those maddening extra steps. I also had to be constantly on the lookout for places where I could jump out of the way of cars racing around the curves. The road was extremely narrow, with scarcely an inch from the white line marking the edge of the road to the hill on my right or the cliff on my left, making safety hard to come by.

Most of the time I walked in the road, ready to move fast when a car swerved around a bend. To make matters worse, poison ivy was abundant all along the way, its tendrils thickly entwined in the roadside manzanita. To avoid it when I paused to rest, just long enough to recover my breath, I balanced on rocks that had rolled down off the hill.

It took all my concentration and willpower to continue on those miserable hills. I climbed and rested, panting my way up the hill, feeling my weight in every step. Frequently I'd look back down the hill, expecting to see that I had made greater strides and accomplished more than it ever turned out I had. Muscles I didn't know I possessed cried out for relief. The new running shoes I had cheerfully counted on soon caused painful blisters on my heels, and my Achilles tendons, stretched to the hilt, felt as if they might snap. Oh, how I longed to be able to shift into a lower gear. And it sure would have helped to have Buck as a playful companion!

But each day I left the house without him. While I was getting ready he would prance around, excited, expecting I'd take him with me. And when I left I didn't dare look back. I didn't want to see those disappointed eyes as he watched me go alone. But my own training took my total attention and exhausted my energy. I couldn't risk Buck's life by training him on this dangerous road until I'd handled it myself.

Every day I did my practice walk on the Calistoga Road, and sometimes I wondered why. But I kept pushing, driving myself to take on more and more of that merciless first hill before turning around and heading back home. And as I climbed, the valley would drop below, making my stomach queasy and my head swim, as my lifelong fear of heights threatened to engulf me. So I devised a way of swinging my body around, not letting my eyes linger on the depth, pulling away fast from the edge.

After a week of this, when summer had rounded the corner and autumn was in the air, one day I had a sensational breakthrough. Suddenly everything seemed to be effortless. I pressed on up Old 20, zipping my way to the top, cresting over the summit. There, feeling on top of the world, I looked out over "16 Percent," the next challenge, thrilling to my sense of achievement.

I continued to work out on Old 20 that way for another week, making fewer and wider loops. I aimed to get Old 20 solidly under my belt before taking on the longer grades of 16 Percent. I'd roll out of bed early in the morning, before Alex and Buck were awake. I'd tiptoe in stocking feet through the house, but I was never quiet enough to get past Buck. He was always at the door, his eagerness and anticipation freshly renewed each day.

My goal was to make it over Old 20 before traffic was heavy and the air filled with exhaust fumes. I'd climb Old 20, continue on to where the road widened and stretched over tawny hills of sun-dried grass, to the St. Helena Junction. A nearby brook threaded its way among the trees. Shafts of light filtered through branches on which the few remaining leaves were turning from rust to gold. After another week, I climbed Old 20 and went on past the junction, waved to horses in a pasture, and walked another two miles as far as the home of the black and white hound that I'd dubbed "Brutus."

Every day Brutus stood on his porch waiting for me, only his yellow eyes moving until I was directly opposite the road from him. Then he would lunge from his platform, growling ferociously, deep in his throat, his snarling lips baring menacing pointed teeth. He seemed always to forget that thirty feet of chain would snap him back by the neck, and so he slashed the air with muddy paws, working himself into a frenzy. "It's me again, Brutus, it's okay," I tried to reassure him. But he always made me nervous, as every day I wondered when the chain might snap. Brutus was part of my training, though I didn't realize it then. Out on the roads of America, Buck and I were to discover that everyone had a dog, it seemed, and, like Brutus, those dogs took their duties seriously. Brutus and I eventually became friends of a sort—or maybe his neck got tired—because after a few weeks he merely lowered his bulky head and snarled.

Two months later my training routine carried me well past the crest of Old 20. I'd swing on past the junction, where I'd wave to the horses who grazed in fields of alfalfa. Another two miles and I'd wave hello to Brutus. Then I'd go on to where, a mile before I got there, I could hear the gobbling jabber of white-feathered turkeys milling around their feed. It reminded me with a pang that Thanksgiving was rapidly approaching. The holidays were not far off, and the departure date was rushing in upon us. There was still so much to do!

This brought me to the downhill part of the road where I thought I'd have it made. Instead, it required braking against the natural pull of gravity, causing different and still-untoned muscles to cry out for mercy. More than once I had to rest on a rock by the side of the road (again braving the poison ivy), and from there I'd look out over the valley. Vineyards lined the hillside, and between the openings in the trees I could see glimpses of the road winding down and into the drowsy town of Calistoga. It seemed so close to me now, and yet so far away. I still couldn't walk the 12.6-mile road nonstop. How could I even consider making a 3,900-mile journey? I was caught up in the nostalgia of leaving, the fear of risk, and the excitement of going. My emotions bounced between joyful eagerness and dismal despair. But I'd pull myself back onto my feet and once again begin the grade slowly, doubling back and forth, again resenting the additional time and steps.

Leaves dried and curled into golden bronze and spiraled to the ground. Squirrels skipped along gnarled and naked branches busily storing away their winter hoard. Then winter blew in with a vengeance, bringing another year of unwanted storms. On some days I stood wistfully at the window, watching the rain pelting the glass. At times like that the pull of home and family was strong. Then I'd thrust my arms into the orange waterproof parka that I'd chosen for its high visibility on the road, and pull on the matching trousers that rustled with every step. (So far these were my only purchases for the journey. My experience with gear was so limited that I didn't know what else to buy. I had to wait until later to determine what I would need.) Because I knew I would face many rainy days and undoubtedly even worse ones than this while out on the road, I made myself step out the door into the downpour.

Storms slam California with a fury. For the second year in a row, winter was violent. In some places the constant torrent of rain flooded towns and stores. Intermittently sodden hillsides broke loose, giving way like volcanic flow, causing mud slides of such magnitude that houses were shoved off their foundations and carried down the hill. But as my eighteen-month walk would take me through two winters, I didn't expect to have rainbows all the way. So I refused to concoct excuses that would get in my way of doing what I really wanted to do, and kept on walking.

Then, one miraculous day, I took both hills without a stop—an entire 12.6 miles without rest. I strode off the backside of 16 Percent, directly into town, and headed straight for a mud-bath spa, where I supported myself on the reception desk and declared to the attendants on duty, "Give me the *works*. I've just walked over from Santa Rosa." The attendants were amazed.

The next day, December 13, 1983, it was my turn to be astonished when the *Calistoga Record* ran the following item: "One of the most familiar faces to Calistoga is Elena Hanuse, a 52-year-old grandmother who regularly walks the 13-mile 16 percent and 20 percent grade hills from Santa Rosa to Calistoga in preparation for further achievements."

I loved the "further achievements."

In late December we celebrated the holiday season with both my boys and their families amid a house in total disarray. Pictures had been taken off the walls and nearly everything was packed away. There were no signs of a holiday in the house after they all left, and I wanted to cram in as much training as possible before I hit the road in earnest. So on Christmas Eve I walked Calistoga Road in one of the most violent storms of the season. There were no streetlamps along the road to light my way. When nightfall came at 4:30, I relied for guidance on the constant stream of headlights and the distant flash of lightning. Rain and wind tore at my parka, which unexpectedly leaked, soaking my clothes and me to the skin. My running shoes were sloshing with water; my toe rubbing against the wet canvas mesh created an unusual squeak. So, concentrating on a rhythmic marching pace, I added the squeak to the beat. Lightning flashed in the distance, sending claps of thunder rolling through the sky. The storm wrenched branches from the trees and hurled them to the ground. Cars streamed by, windshield wipers on high, headlights piercing the dark. Abruptly a yellow compact swerved off the road and pulled to a stop just ahead of me. A young woman cranked down her window and stuck her head out into the howling rain.

"Do you need help?" she screamed, blinking rapidly to clear her eyes.

"No, thank you." I tried to wave her on, but she waited.

"What are you doing out here?" she demanded, her blond hair slapping wildly in the rain.

"Walking." It sounded flimsy even to my ears.

"We saw you hours ago. We thought your car broke down!"

I could tell she was trying to make sense of an incomprehensible situation. She was young, sweet, and convinced I needed help.

"I'm in training," I said, as though that would explain, although I knew immediately that it wouldn't, not to this young lady.

"For what?" she asked incredulously. After all, what could a fifty-two-year-old lady, walking in a violent storm, after dark, on Christmas Eve, possibly be training for?

So I went for it. "A walk across America." It was my first attempt at saying it to a stranger, and it sounded awkward, but her face lit up with astonishment and admiration.

"No kidding!" she said. She turned to her companion to make certain he'd heard. He had, and he leaned forward to look at me. "This is my husband, Ted. I'm Karen." She rushed through the introduction to ask, "When are you leaving?" Her face expressed wonder and, yes, even respect. Karen and I had made a connection.

They were both smiling broadly; clearly they approved. "Can we get you anything?" she asked, and I felt that if at the moment I had wanted a full-course turkey dinner with all the fixings, they would have found a way to get it and maybe even have stayed to share it with me.

"No, thanks. I'm really okay, but I'd better get moving; I'm getting pretty cold out here."

Ted reached out his hand. "Merry Christmas," he said earnestly.

"God bless you," Karen said, each word spoken with emphasis, warmth, and pride.

I stood and watched them wave until they disappeared down the road into the night, and their cheer stayed with me, wrapping me in a glow of well-being. I didn't know it then, but Karen and Ted were the first of countless others who would rally behind my venture into America, who would get caught up in the spirit of achievement and patriotic cheer, and would be my supporters when my spirits flagged.

Alex was waiting for me in Calistoga, standing in the halo of a lamppost entwined with golden Christmas tinsel that shimmered in the wind. Storefronts were joyously decorated in holiday cheer, and the soft music of carols carried through the streets. He wrapped a warm jacket around my shoulders and eased me into the car. My hair was soaked and plastered against my head, and water dribbled down my forehead, running over my brows. Alex drove to the Mount View Inn, where he'd found a roaring log fire in the lobby. I crouched as close as I dared to the flames leaping about in the open hearth, letting my clothes dry on my body while Alex brought us a brandy to share. This was it; we both knew it. We raised the snifter, and the fire flickered on the amber liquid. We toasted each other and my walk across America. In that moment we said good-bye to the life we'd known and hello to the unknowns ahead. We were ready to go.

Ready to go? Well, almost! There is always something more to do. But we were as ready as we were ever going to be. We had put the house up for lease; the furniture would go into storage. These tasks were entrusted to Violet, a very capable and loving friend.

But deciding what to take with us was the biggest remaining challenge.

One week before we left home and after giving it much thought, we bought the two-tone brown R.V., and in his usual upbeat way, Alex promptly named it "Home Sweet Home." After a swift look around the very compact living areas and laughing ourselves silly about how we'd crowd what we'd need into it, we began deciding what we could take with us. We quickly realized that it wouldn't be much. On the Sunday before we left, we began loading the camper for departure.

While the R.V.'s interior was ingeniously laid out, storage space was seriously limited. With just three minuscule plastic bedroom drawers available to me, I packed only several fleece warm-up suits, two pairs of heavy-duty sneakers, and one special dress. I discovered later that I forgot to pack the shoes that went with it.

Home Sweet Home was cozy, cramped, and self-contained. That meant it had everything we'd need to be independent in areas where we couldn't find electricity and running water. That is, if we remembered to buy gas—which the vehicle drank like a hog—and filled the small water-holding tank. Theoretically we could be in the middle of a desert and still be able to wash, cook, and read. A generator belched out volumes of noise and exhaust but produced electricity. However, on the road we'd soon learn that the noise of the generator so violated the serenity of mountain meadows that we tried not to use it. The camper also had a very, very mini-bathroom with not an inch to spare, but it was equipped with a basin, a toilet, and even a shower. Taking a shower meant measuring by the cupful the amount of water used. I would learn to be a master at taking the hose and rinsing down fast, soaping up faster, and then rinsing again—but oh so sparingly and oh so quickly! During the winter, especially when it was so chilly that icicles hung from the bumper, showering was a bone-shivering process indeed.

At the rear of Home Sweet Home a cubbyhole with a full-sized bed served as a bedroom, but there was no room to get around the bed. Whoever went to bed first would either have to sleep next to the window or risk being climbed over. The cooking area was in the middle of the R.V. It had a stainless-steel sink, a four-burner gas stove with oven, and a refrigerator, all scaled down to doll-house size. As neither of us was likely to be doing a lot of baking, I converted the oven into a desk where I stored envelopes, postage stamps, pens, and pencils, things I needed in order to stay in contact with family and friends, and eventually to respond to the hundreds of letters we started to receive from the huge network of new friends we made along the way. We had arranged for a friend to pick them up each day at a post office box in Santa Rosa and reroute them to General Delivery in a town I would be walking toward.

It didn't take much to see that if either Alex or I were to stir a stew on the stove, there wouldn't be a hair's breadth of room in the kitchen for anyone else. Home Sweet Home seemed awkwardly crowded to us at first. Two adults and one hefty dog confined in less than two hundred square feet? One of us was bound to be in the way of another at all times. And that proved to be true. Buck didn't help at all. Until he grew used to our new and strange living conditions, he padded around endlessly, sniffing into every crevice and corner, making certain that things were as they should be before he'd finally curl up into a ball, always as close as he could get to our feet. As a result he was constantly in the way. At home Buck slept on his oval rug on the carpeted floor, and we took the rug along for him. At first he followed that routine in the R.V., but when we noticed him shivering on the drafty, thinly insulated floorboards, we broke a rule and gave him the privilege of sleeping on the couch. When he continued to shiver, we put a long T-shirt on him at night. He knew what it was for, and he welcomed it. On the coldest winter nights Buck would drag out his "nightgown" and wait for one of us to put it on him.

The living room, which consisted of Buck's couch and two matching chairs, was at the front end of the R.V. That's where we put the computer. At first we set it impractically on one end of the couch, but when Guy, my younger son, saw how inconvenient that was, he came up with an ingenious solution. He whipped out a tape measure and made a few calculations. The following weekend he came after us on the road, and over the engine housing between the driver's and passenger's seats, installed a three-shelved console he'd built. That unit stacked Alex's computer, keyboard, and monitor neatly. We added a high stool, and Alex was in business.

In the end we left home with practically nothing: a few books, a few pieces of clothing, a few pots and pans, two favorite blue china dinner plates (a token touch of refinement), and Buck's bowls. And it was positively amazing to discover how little we needed to get by and be happy.

Late in the evening of January 3, we finally stood by our front door at home, exhausted to the bones. "That's it?" Alex looked to me for confirmation. He pulled a switch and the house went dark. My heart thumped and I took another moment to look around. I knew what I'd miss most. In the shadows I could see the outline of my grand piano and beyond it the flower boxes Alex had kept blooming. The tender green spikes of daffodils and tulips were already beginning to show.

"Ready?" Alex asked softly, and then pulled the door closed and turned the key, and we climbed into the camper and headed down the driveway. It didn't help either of us one bit when Buck whimpered sorrowfully as the house disappeared from view.

We drove the camper 50 miles south to the north end of the Golden Gate Bridge. There, in the Vista Point parking area, Alex positioned the camper so that in the morning, when I first opened my eyes, I'd see the skyline of the city I've always called home. A gauzy fog lay over the highest spires, and the lights on the bridges crossing the bay stretched out like strings of jewels. Just before I drifted off to sleep I thought with a sudden pang: I've burned all my bridges. There's really no turning back now. But I snuggled down deeper because I didn't want to, anyhow.

TWO

·········•••••·••••·•·•••••·•••••••••••••·

Going the Wrong Way

The wind whipped the collar of my jacket, nicking and stinging my cheeks. My pants stretched across my shins and flapped madly behind my calves. The wind gusted from the ocean so fiercely that I had to lean into it to keep my balance. High on the Golden Gate Bridge 220 feet above the waters of the turbulent Pacific, suspended by cold massive steel cables, I was afraid, and my fear of height threatened to overpower me. My hands were clammy and my mind dwelled upon the open space below. At times I felt an inexplicable pull dragging me over the rail. I looked south (the bridge is less than a mile long). I saw the span arch and disappear and thought to myself, if I can only get that far, which is half the distance across the Golden Gate, if I can walk that half of the bridge, I know I can do the rest.

I was dizzy; the bridge swayed and the wind tore at me. I might as well get on with it. My friends stood awkwardly waiting for me to go, making talk with well-meant advice:

"Be careful."

"Call if you need anything."

"Don't forget to use a sunscreen."

One of my last hugs was for Alice, a friend through thick and thin. We'd known each other forever, it seemed, and I knew that no matter what, she'd be there in the end.

There was nothing more to say, and my well-wishers were cold. Buck was shivering, too. His stubby red hair covers muscles built for action, not for standing around. He kept pulling back from the rail. He doesn't like high places either. There was only one way to do this and that was to go. Guy, my younger son, put his arms around me and held me for a long, warm hug, the sound of his voice close to my ear. "Go for it, Mom." Gary, his older brother, hugged me tightly and rocked me back and forth a little. "Don't forget to call, Mom," he said.

The foghorns sounded mournful warnings in the bay, adding to the sorrow of departure. The fog was dense, sliding noiselessly over the bridge's span, plunging into the channel below. Suddenly I moved forward, Buck at my heels, and we didn't look back. We were off! Only 3,900 miles to go!

It was strangely exhilarating to be moving freely across the span, buffeted by the wind, just where my dream had been born so many years before. Early morning joggers jostled past and I hugged my treasured adventure like a private secret down deep inside, feeling the privacy and independence of the moment. I knew what I wanted to do. I was acting upon my instincts, reaching out to others. That was something I'd always known but this was a bigger reach, stretching across the continent. If along the way I touched some others, stirring again what beats inside the heart of each of us, then my walk would have served its purpose.

Buck walked carefully to avoid the cracks between sections of the bridge road. When I dared to look through those breaks, I could see the channel waters crashing thunderously against the concrete piers. Those concrete structures gave rise to the two majestic towers from which the bridge is suspended. As I walked by, a crew on scaffolding was sandblasting the sea-weather corrosion from the bridge's monumental frame. I looked out over the commuter traffic rushing south into the city, out to the Pacific horizon where a few fishing boats, tossing on the waves, were heading out to sea for the salmon, trailed by sea gulls wheeling behind in anticipation of the catch.

And then, as I had forty-six years before, I turned to the east. The fog was lifting, the sun breaking through, and I looked out across the blue of the bay where white sails leaned into the wind, swinging around Alcatraz Island. I gazed into the distance, toward my country, thrilled finally to be on my way.

At the tollgate that leads off the bridge and to the Presidio, I pushed through the turnstile and held it while Bucky trotted through; then we turned right into the Presidio. Many years ago it had been a Spanish military post that protected the Mission of St. Francis. Now it is the headquarters of the Sixth U.S. Army. I tried to slip Buck past the barracks unnoticed, but a group of soldiers called out to him, "Hey, pooch, where you goin'?" and Buck ran to them. They made a big fuss over him and naturally he loved it. We turned into Golden Gate Park and followed a bridle path out to the Great Highway. The eucalyptus trees dripped their leaves upon us, scenting the air. I had intended to walk the highway but sand covered it with mini-dunes, so we took the beach side of Forty-eighth Avenue instead.

I knew these streets so well. After all, San Francisco is my hometown. Yet an uncommon sense of anonymity and unusual freedom marked my steps. With an undercurrent of eagerness for adventure and discovery I felt a lighthearted and free wheeling buoyancy pushing me along.

I let Buck run free, and he disappeared into the underbrush. I could tell where he was because I saw leaves shaking and heard twigs snap. When he came back to check up on me, I sent him off again. I knew I would have to keep him close once we hit the country's highways, and I wanted him to enjoy his sense of freedom just as I was enjoying mine.

By midafternoon we had covered the roughly nine miles to the southwest corner of the city, and there, at the zoo, we turned up Skyline Boulevard. Skyline would carry us over the San Mateo hills and through Daly City, only six miles from the coast. A little farther at San Bruno I'd take Highway 82 down to the coastal highway, which I wanted to follow. A man was trudging down the road toward me, pushing one foot in front of the other with not much commitment in his steps. His thin white hair wandered loosely in the breeze and his windbreaker was zipped up to protect a lean stubbled chin. "Hello," I called to him from a polite distance. He continued to advance steadily; his blue-gray eyes measured me, but he did not acknowledge my greeting. There was no pedestrian lane here, so one of us had to step off the road to let the other by. He didn't and neither did I, so we stopped, facing each other.

"You're a long way from somewhere," I said as an opening.

"You are, too," he challenged.

I refused to be put off by the reticence in his tone. "I know this area very well. It's quite a walk from anyplace around here." I was ready to be friendly.

He sighed and resigned himself to answer, as though responding was a great burden. "Five years ago I lost my wife. Then I had a heart attack. I do this every day to keep my sanity. What about you?"

Bolstered by my encounter with Karen and Ted, I said, with confidence this time, "I've just started a transcontinental walk across America. I'm heading for New York City."

He studied me for a long moment, then, without responding, he lowered his head and detoured around me. But with just a thin trace of humor showing on his lips, he called back over his shoulder, "You're going the wrong way!"

He made me laugh, but of course it was true. Since I was leaving in winter, and the road over the Sierra Nevada directly east of San Francisco was impassable, my route was circuitous. Tioga Pass was blocked by winter snow. Therefore, to find a passage over the Sierras at this time of year I had to go 300 miles south before I could begin to take my first steps east. Coast to coast the continental mileage was tremendous, even if I could have walked it as the bird flies, but walking 300 miles south when I needed to go east? I preferred not to think about it.

Buck and I continued on Skyline Boulevard, hugging the narrow edge of the road while cars swept dangerously close on our right. But the shoulder of the road was planted with clumps of ice plant, a thick, crawling, succulent ground cover. Its dense wandering roots help to keep the shifting sand in place, but its lumpy surface caused me to stumble, so we walked on the fringe of it. Row upon row of almost identical stucco houses marched off to the ocean cliffs only a few miles away, where blustery Pacific winds pound and erode the bluffs. Some of those houses were perched precariously close to the crumbling edge. More than one had already had its foundation undermined and had tumbled over the side. Other residents continued to stay, hoping it wouldn't happen to them.

The damp ocean wind carried the smell of salt and left a briny deposit on my lips. The wind also worked under my jacket and up my sleeves, chilling me to the bone. I pulled my cap closer over my ears and hunched deeper into my all-weather jacket. A continual stream of cars went ripping by. I turned my head frequently, nervously looking over my shoulder, relieved to see Buck's shadow following on my heels right behind.

We climbed steadily, looking down into the backyards of pastel-colored row houses. The vivid red and turquoise trim on some of them reflected the recent immigration of Asiatics into this area. San Francisco has always been home to distinctive and friendly ethnic communities—Italian, Russian, Chinese, and ever so many more. And each brought with them their own special customs, which have helped to make "the City" one of the fascinating cosmopolitan centers of the world. Most recently the Bay Area had been absorbing enormous numbers of people from Vietnam, Korea, and Samoa, and of course their unique cultural customs had accompanied them. Looking down into the yard of one of these typically middle-class homes, I saw an example of these customs. Tethered to a stake by a short rope around his neck, a goat stood in the center of a small patch of lawn. Long-term residents in this neighborhood had frequently been upset of late when newly arrived residents barbecued goats in open backyard pits, or, worse, when family dogs and cats mysteriously disappeared.

Sixteen miles south of San Francisco, a storm lashed us with a fury. It rolled in from the ocean, blackening the sky, carrying with it a deluge so formidable it seemed it could drown the state. Streets were flooded, gutters ran like rivers, and traffic moved at a crawl. Way up ahead I could make out a detour and a highway patrolman in a long yellow rubber coat, turning cars back one by one. He was dimly profiled within the lights of amber barricade blinkers and a rotating, red police light that pulsated into the night. I cupped my hands around my mouth and shouted into the storm, "What's the problem?"

"Landslide. This road is closed to traffic." He looked at me for a brief moment, never once losing his attention to the traffic.

"I'm walking. Can I get through?" I yelled.

"Nobody can," he hollered back. "That whole area out there, Devil's Slide, just dropped into the ocean. Anybody out there at the time went along with it. We're turning all traffic around."

"I've got a camper coming along. I need a place to park it."

"That center over there." His right arm continued making rotations, and his left pointed in the direction of a shopping center. "Looks like you could put it there. I'll send the local police over, they'll be able to help."

"Thanks," I called out. He had given me the information I needed. Now I needed to locate Alex, who probably was on his way to pick us up. He had told me that he would meet us on the coastal highway right after Pacifica, on the very part of the road that had vanished into the Pacific Ocean. It was part of our plan to park the camper out there overnight and get some sleep before Buck and I hit the road again early in the morning. I had no way to tell Alex about the detour, but he'd obviously find out by himself and look for us. The best thing to do was to wait by the detour on the side of the road. That way he couldn't miss us.

Buck and I sat on the curb by the side of the road and watched the officer as he turned the long line of vehicles around. What else could we do? We couldn't go inside one of the shops—Alex would never find us—so we had no other option but to wait it out on the curb. Buck was agitated by the rain, frequently shaking himself, flinging water off into the air. His stubby hair offered little protection, and he had no experience waiting out storms. He darted one way and then another in an attempt to get away from the drops that pelted him. So I took off one of my layers—my red-hooded sweat-shirt—and poked his feet down into the sleeves, rolling up the cuffs and drawing the hood snugly over his ears. Then I laughed out loud. He looked as if he were in costume, ready to play the part of the wolf in Little Red Riding Hood. But soon he was soaked again.

While our muscles chilled in our soggy clothes, I had time to think about the strangeness of my situation. How had I appeared to that officer? Like an eccentric, a kook? Here I sat, a lady with a dog in a red-hooded sweatshirt who wanders about in a howling storm and announces that she's walking. I got to giggling about it. Meanwhile I watched the policeman with admiration. I thought it quite amazing how he handled the traffic efficiently, all the while ready to respond courteously to problems and situations as diverse—even strange—as mine. He fit right in with my lifetime image of responsible police service. Later I would encounter one who did not measure up to that image.

After what seemed like an eternity, I saw the camper inching along in the long line of vehicles backed up over the hill. "Come on, Buck, let's go!" We ran the half mile and I yelled to Alex through the window, "We can't go that way. The road is gone. That officer up ahead suggests we spend the night in the shopping center."

Alex pulled out of line and into the parking lot, where we found a location away from the other vehicles parked there. I pulled off my wet shoes and was examining the new blisters unexpectedly forming on my heels when a loud bang on the side of the camper startled us. Outside were two policeman in raincoats slick with rain. "Evening, ma'am. That highway patrolman over there said you're looking for a place to stay?" Their eyes swiftly searched the inside of the camper. What were they looking for? Could I be harboring drugs? A fifty-two-year-old grandmother in fleece? I bit my lip so as not to smile. Who could blame them for "checking me out"?

"Looks like this is as good a place as any," said one of the officers. They continued their probe, efficiently and politely, trying to determine what I could be about.

All the while, the officers were courteous. "The other officer said you were walking. Is that what you're doing?" It was evident that they thought my situation clearly on the bizarre side, though their swift scan had produced nothing odd, excepting Buck, who was still wearing his wolf outfit.

"I left San Francisco this morning planning to take the coast road south, when I ran into the detour," I said matter-of-factly, as though this were a scene they might encounter on any day. "I'm on a cross-country walk, across America. I need a place to spend the night before rerouting."

Something in my demeanor convinced them and immediately their expressions relaxed. "You are?" They extended their help by glancing around the lot behind them, looking for a better location for us. "Look, why don't you pull over closer to that lamppost? The extra light can't hurt. And don't worry, we'll come by during the night just to make sure everything's okay. You need your sleep." They stepped back to leave. "Night, ma'am," they said a little self-consciously, because they were young—I could have been their mother—and I sensed they could hardly contain their enthusiasm, which might mar their concept of police dignity. Then, touching the top of their caps, "Get a good night's rest—and good luck, too."

There it was again, the demeanor that revealed imaginations fired up by the concept of my journey across America. I was going beyond the usual, and by doing it I was living out a shared collective dream.

Buck and I were exhausted. The unexpected detour, the storm, the first day's miles and adventures, all of these had taken their toll. Across the lot, the warm red glow of a pizza sign beckoned. It was an invitation Alex and I couldn't ignore. For our first day on the road I'd stuffed my pockets with nuts and fruit, which I'd finished long ago, and some large dog biscuits, which Buck had wolfed down almost within the first hour. At this point a pizza seemed a fantastic idea, and besides, the pizzeria was the only place around still open.

The pizza parlor was empty except for the man at the counter who was emptying the till. He looked up and seemed surprised and somewhat annoyed to see us. "What brings you out in this kind of weather?" he exclaimed. "I was just about to close." It was a suggestion to leave.

"We've just come down from San Francisco and got as far as the roadblock. I'm on a walk across America heading for New York City and"—here I hesitated—" I have a special request." He waited with a show of bored and impatient detachment. It had been a long time since this man had really connected with anyone, and he had his "no" ready and waiting for me. "My dog and I were caught in that storm out there. I know he's not allowed in here, but he's damp and I hate to make him wait outside. There's no one else in here," I said, looking around to make my point, "and it's late, and you're not likely to have an inspection on this kind of night, anyway." Then I went for it. "Could I bring him inside?" The man's eyebrows lifted. "I'll keep him under the table," I promised, "and if he's a problem I'll take him right back outside."

Buck was looking through the glass door. He tilted his head to one side and lifted his ears entreatingly, the short stub of his tail wagging in hopeful anticipation. The man looked at Buck and sighed a reluctant resignation. I'm sure he didn't even understand why himself, but his "no" had been dissolved.

"Okay," he grumbled, and he wrote down our food order. "Have a seat. I'll bring your pizza over when it's ready." But I noticed him casting sidewise glances at us while he stretched the round of dough and sent it spinning into the air.

Along with the pizza, he set down two beers we hadn't ordered. Then he reached behind him for a chair, spun it around on one leg, and sat down backward, resting his chin on his arms across the back. He looked at me for a long moment. "My name's Bob," he started, "and I'd like to ask you a question. Why?" It was more like a challenge than a question.

I sensed that Bob's "Why?" was deep and searching, more than he wanted to let on. Everything about this man showed that he'd given up a long time ago and was merely going through the motions of life. But he'd sensed, accurately, that my walk was much more for me than just being able to say I could do it. What Bob hungered to hear was a validation for living and the meaning of life.

I was starving and just beginning to get warm, but I put the pizza down.

"Bob," I began, and was suddenly uncomfortable. I found that I was unprepared to answer his question. So I hedged: "Let me think about it while I eat."

I began to eat, not really thinking about what I was putting into my mouth, and my thoughts ran backward, back to the child of six standing on the bridge with my mother, knowing I could reach out to my country. Even at that time, I had a strong desire to include everyone in the world that was mine, and when others would sometimes try to persuade me to join against someone else, I couldn't do it. I liked people the way they were, even if they were different, and amid our differences, the most natural connections were made between us.

I was nine when I began to study music, and for many years I was willing to follow my mother's dream that I become a classical musician. I studied first the violin and piano, and later the cello and the larger bass viol. It was my intention to communicate with people through music, feeling then as I do now that music is the closest we have to a universal language. Music isn't as precise as the spoken word, however, and the time came when what I wanted more than anything else was a clearer way to express myself.

But I set that dream aside for a while, and instead focused on doing what others expected of me. I married young, and my husband and I did all the things we were expected to do. We bought a new car, then a new house, and within five years had added two sons. He went to work and I kept the house and that was the sum total of life. Except that, although I couldn't identify it or speak of it then, there was a persistent hunger, a deep uncompromising yearning, to have my life mean more. So one day I took a step in the direction of doing what I longed to do. I went out to the San Francisco City College and signed up for a course in the humanities. Suddenly I was living again in a world of thought, ideas, and words. It was exciting and expanding, and the following semester I signed up for more classes. My actions did nothing to strengthen our marriage, however. We had so few ways of communicating with one another, and neither of us knew how to open up more. I gradually came to the conclusion that the best thing for me to do was to leave. I had to find my way alone again.

But that took years of vacillation. I agonized over being irresistibly drawn toward a greater expression of myself but yielding to the pressures to conform and then undergoing the torment of trying to reconcile the two. But my conflict inevitably led to the next frightening step. One day I went to see a lawyer.

On that somber day I climbed the dark wooden steps to the attorney's second-floor office. After waiting for what seemed an eternity, I was ushered into his presence. He slowly raised his head from the papers he was reviewing, pushed his glasses higher on his ruddy nose, and bent his head to peer at me over the gold frames. After studying me for a few moments, he asked with a scowl, "What can I do for you?"

I almost fled. "I—I—want a divorce," I said so timidly that he couldn't hear me—at least he didn't answer—so I cleared my throat and tried again. "I want a divorce."

He pushed back in his chair.

"What are your grounds?"

I couldn't answer.

"Does your husband mistreat you?"

"No."

"Do you have a roof over your head?"

"Yes."

"And food in your mouth?"

"Yes."

"Then go home and be grateful for a husband who does all that. You don't need a divorce; you need humility."

For two more years I sidestepped my personal dreams and

truly tried hard not to be unhappy. I doubled my classes and entered the education program at San Francisco State University. I took my children to class with me when I had to and studied when they napped or were in school. I kept the house in perfect order and my studies out of sight. But now I had a mission. I would be a teacher. I would support myself and my children that way and at the same time work with young people, opening them to their own worth and potential. One year before I graduated cum laude, having consistently been on the dean's list, I received a student loan and a scholarship and used that money to seek a lawyer a second time. I chose more carefully this time. She did not ask why I wanted a divorce.

So it was that twelve months later, with my degree proudly in hand, I moved my children and myself to Monterey County, about one hundred miles south of San Francisco, accepting an offer to teach there. Our snug country home was set among a grove of pine trees in the middle of eleven pastoral acres and it had an enormous log-burning stone fireplace. The timbered porch overlooked the beautiful, serene Salinas Valley, and for me our new home was straight out of heaven. I was happy; my life had again taken on meaning.

While my children attended their rural school I took on my assignment of teaching thirty-five third graders. From my student teaching days I was aware of the influence a teacher can have upon students, and I wanted to be the best I could. I wanted those youngsters to go beyond what I had to offer and to be the best—not better than someone else, but each of them to be his and her very own best. And as it often happens, as new teacher on the staff I got the most difficult group in the school.

Most of those children hated to come to class. Stomach-aches and bed-wetting and a multitude of other problems were commonplace among them. But I loved them and they knew it, and as a result my job was made easier, because they tried so hard to please in return. I had no favorites; they were all my favorites, but it took them a while to sort out their feelings about that. The slowest ones learned, the fastest ones learned, and they all found an acceptance for each other that was unfamiliar to them. They even discovered that they'd rather be in school than any other place, so they began showing up early and hanging around the classroom door until I let them in. Then they stayed late and I had to chase them home.

I showed them how to be resourceful and responsible by selling lemonade and cookies at recess. They raised enough money to plant a small plot of ground in front of the school. We all walked to a nearby nursery where the children chose junipers and lobelia, which they planted with shovels and trowels they brought from home. Their efforts got them on the television news and in the newspaper and they felt good about what they'd achieved. They even had money left over to send to the City of Hope. On a map we traced the journey of that hospital ship as it traveled from port to port, making a contribution of health to other nations. They saw how, by participating with others, they could have an effect upon the world—even if they were only eight years old. Of course they learned to read and write and do arithmetic as well as to draw what they saw, write what they thought, and to love doing it.

Another year I was given an assignment to work with youngsters who had more serious behavior problems. I loved them, too, and they knew it. I don't mean that I loved their aggressive behavior; rather, I loved the really great kids buried under all the acquired bravado. Those kids, too, found out that school could be the kind of place where they wanted to be. One day, however, something shocking happened. The principal walked into my class and pointed a finger at one of my students, Marty, who obediently followed him out of the classroom. From the other side of the closed door we heard the spanking. The door opened and Marty was shoved back inside, blinking back the tears smarting in his eyes.

"What did he do?" I asked incredulously.

"Nothing," the principal said as he looked around at the

rest of the youngsters. "Just let that be a reminder, in case any of you think you want to get out of line."

I was appalled. I have too much respect for young people to manipulate them like that. I respect them even when they are insolent, preferring to correct them by my example rather than by joining them in disrespect. I probably felt that walloping more deeply than Marty did, and I knew that inside the education system I would find more educators like that than I wanted to see. I resigned and moved to Denver, Colorado, encouraged by the recommendation of a friend, plus the attraction of adventure in a completely new environment. I now had firmly in mind the intention of opening my own school.

In any school it seems there are always a few youngsters of good intelligence who apear unable to learn through normal procedures. Often they are bright. Sometimes they are even gifted, as it was with Einstein, who was so withdrawn that it was thought he could never be a success. But when it happens that the right connection is made with young people like that, it is always a great satisfaction to see what they can become. I'd taken a special interest in children such as this, so once I reached Denver I headed back to school to do graduate work in this area.

The school I established on Capitol Hill had as its primary purpose to reinstate children's natural ability to feel good about themselves and others. There's no mystery about this process. The link that ignites their interest is formed through love and respect. The real mystery is that sometimes we forget it. But it happens as surely as night follows day that if children feel safe and appreciated, they will naturally behave lovably. It's that simple: you can love anybody into being lovable. Eventually they will come of their own accord to the realization that they are respectable and will want to act that way. When instead we do the opposite and treat a person—child or adult—as unlovable, we lock them into that kind of behavior.

Something marvelous happens when we help others grow.

Without even looking for it, love inevitably comes back to us and we find ourselves flourishing as fast as those we're helping. It's a win-win situation for all—a law of nature. A seed wants to grow.

My walk was only another track I was taking in order to continue my own expansion, always with the intention of giving it to others, of sharing what I learned with them. I didn't know what I would learn—there's no curriculum that reveals what eighteen months on the roads of America would turn up—and I knew even less what form my own return offering would take.

Bob was listening patiently as I explained aloud some of what I had been thinking, and it was then I saw a spark in his eyes:

"I've felt like that," he said. I could almost see his mind doing calculations as he continued, "How long do you figure this walk will take?"

There it was: Bob, too, had dreams, and it was clear that for him I represented the hope, the possibility, that perhaps one day he could realize his own dreams.

There was so much more to say and I was exhausted. Thankfully Bucky saved the day, making a wide-mouthed noisy yawn. He, too, was tired. I could see that the conversation might have gone on all night, but it seemed enough right now for me to know I had touched someone, and for Bob to know that dreams, even difficult ones, come true.

Bob was standing now, making ready to leave. "You wanna know something? Two years ago I sold this place, after I'd built it up from nothing." He stood up straighter, a bit of pride showing. "But the guy I sold it to ran it into the ground. I couldn't just let it go. I had to come back." He waited somewhat defensively for an unfavorable reaction, but when none came, he confided his truth to me. "I like it here. The people all know me. They come in and call me by name.

That makes you feel good. Together my wife and I spent years building this up." A broad smile came to his face. "And that's when we were happiest! When we were doing something."

He stood up with more energy than he'd shown before. He looked me straight in the eye, and before I could realize what he was doing, he had taken out his wallet and stuffed ten dollars into my pocket. It would have been rude to return it. "Lady," he said, "I want to sign your jacket." And he did, with renewed confidence and a bold-hearted flourish.

THREE

······.····..·.······.·.··.·.·······..·

Learning the Hard Way

The next morning, after the storm, Alex rerouted us away from the coast, since Highway 1 was still closed to traffic. We backed up onto the San Mateo hills where we continued on along Skyline Boulevard. From there I looked down on the serene oak-studded hillsides and the sparkling San Andreas Reservoir, marveling that this peaceful countryside concealed the violently destructive San Andreas Fault, that treacherous break in the earth's crust that in 1906 had shaken San Francisco to rubble.

I still wanted to walk along the coast, so a few miles farther we again turned off to the right at Highway 92, crossing the dam at Crystal Spring Lake. We climbed Montara Mountain before beginning the winding descent down to the seaside community of Half Moon Bay. The rain was with us again, sweeping up the narrow road. Eucalyptus trees lining the road had dropped a blanket of seedpods so thick I couldn't avoid stepping on them. They rolled under my feet, repeatedly jerking me off balance.

Two days later we were again following the Pacific coast. I figured that as long as I had to head south for the winter, I might as well travel the roads of greatest beauty. This one in particular had special meaning for me. When Gary and Guy were small and I was studying for my teaching degree at the university, I frequently brought them here, where the bluffs slope gently, forming protected inlets and shallow tide pools. We'd examine these pools together, searching for sea anemone, hermit crabs, and other sea animals that make their homes in the rocky ocean crevices. Then I'd leave them to their own explorations, while I sat on the rocks where I could watch them and studied for exams. These tide pools were a way to share the natural balance of things. Years later, when Alex and I had decided to marry and discovered that we both knew and loved this place, we made our commitment at the edge of the Pacific, on those same ocean-washed rocks in Pescadero.

I would have liked to share these memories with Alex, but he was off in the camper at Santa Cruz, forty miles away, and I wouldn't see him before nightfall. I found a clump of calla lilies growing on the side of the road, so I slipped my fingers deep into the tightly wound leaves and broke off a single elegant stem. That night I sketched the lily, and it became the first of a collection of drawings I'd make along the way. I'd known all along that I'd miss Alex's gardens, but nature's more than made up for them. Even in the deserts, flowers were scattered in profusion along the way.

Eighty-two miles and six blisters south of San Francisco I arrived at Santa Cruz. In the camper I had propped a relief map of America along the top of Buck's couch, and that night, while pulling off my socks, I noticed that the mileage Buck and I had already walked was actually observable on the map! What a surprise. We'd done 82 measurable miles! I quickly figured, "Buck and I just have to do that distance 48 more times, and we'll be in New York." I was really excited by that idea and began to count the continental mileage in 82-mile segments.

Between the blisters on my feet and the sometimes seemingly endless segments left to go, I needed to maintain my courage. It was then I remembered another time in my life when I learned that a challenge which might otherwise seem impossible could be managed.

That time I had been on a mountain. It was in the winter of 1964 that I had gone to Heavenly Valley, a spectacular ski resort near the shores of Lake Tahoe in northern California. I was with a small group of close friends who were good skiers. I wasn't, but that didn't matter to them. They were more than willing to give me some great skiing tips. It was the end of a strenuous day on the slopes and I had made encouraging progress, so I decided to take one more last run by myself. I plowed my way to the nearest lift and held my breath while I was carried to the top of the hill.

I heard the clankity-clankity of meshing gears grow louder. My skis dangled heavily from my boots. At the top of the lift I bolted from my seat, landed with a smack on the ice-slicked ramp, and careened to a powdery stop. I looked around. Nobody else was up there. It was late in the day and the magnitude of the mountain surrounded me with an awesome silence. A stirring of apprehension crept over my chest, so I pushed off, reckless in my haste, and unexpectedly found myself looking straight down Gun Barrel, the most treacherous run on the mountain. It was foolhardy to think I could ski those sheer edges and vertical cliffs. I searched frantically for a sign pointing to the beginner or even the intermediate slope. It didn't exist. Desperately I scanned the hills for someone to save me, to get me out of there. But there was no one, only the snow-burdened conifers standing in silent observation. The sky was quickly closing in, blurring the landscape, erasing shadows so that I couldn't tell how high the bumps were or how deep the holes in the run. Raw fear gnawed the edges of my ribs. Staring down that vertical slope, I knew I could not handle it.

Wind burst across the mountain, whipping powder into a furious explosion around me. Away down the mountain I isolated a tree. Elena, I asked myself, can you ski that far? Boulders projected menacingly from the snow-packed surface. I knew there was no way I could maneuver my skis that far. Closer, a stunted pine clung precariously from a crevice. Again I searched myself. Can you ski that far? No, the answer came within. There's no way I can handle my skis that well. Well, Elena, can you handle the first ten feet of that mountain? Yes, ten feet I can handle. And the next ten feet? Yes, that I can handle. Well, then, get going, because you have a mountain to handle, ten feet at a time. And it worked.

Twenty years later, crossing the continent on foot seemed as impossible a venture as my skiing Gun Barrel. But as I had once handled the mountain, so I was taking in America—one step at a time.

With some regret we left the awesome Pacific coast, heading inland toward the Santa Cruz Mountains. We crossed through Watsonville, a rural artichoke-growing community with a wide main street and many franchised food chains. We then stayed on Highway 152, until from a distance the road seemed to come to an end at the foot of a mountain. On the other side of that mountain we'd come to Gilroy, the Garlic Capital of the World.

Buck and I had an 18-mile itinerary for the day. We would take the road that climbed Madonna Mountain. Those mountain passages were milestones to me, but at a mere 1,309 feet above sea level Hecker Pass was just a baby compared with what was in store.

We left the wide-open, flat-country fields, where miles of winter vegetables were growing in precise rows, and entered the random growth of a redwood forest, where lush ferns and shady groves of stately redwoods and a brook surrounded us with a different density of vegetation. The road was steep, so I welcomed the wooded terrain for which Old 20 had prepared me well. Buck ran through the forest, leaping fallen logs, having the time of his life inhaling odors he had never encountered before. There was almost no traffic, so the solitude of the quiet woods was ours alone to enjoy. I saw a banana slug creeping across the road, swooped him up with a leaf, and put him on a fern frond to feed.

When we had climbed approximately one-third of the ascent, the road became sharper, steeper, and the trees on the cliffside were no longer tall enough to cover the view of the valley. Far out, over the trees and across the valley, was the Pacific Ocean. We continued with very few stops, once to gather wildflowers—they would make the cramped camper seem more like home—and another while Buck ran to the brook. I sat down on a log to wait for him and to drink a carton of orange juice I had brought with me.

But there was to be no rest for me. Alex was waiting at the summit, and was now in view, making arm gestures in order to encourage me to hurry the last steps. "I'm taking you to Gilroy right now. A school wants you to talk to an assembly at one o'clock and we'll barely make it."

Bucky and I jumped into the car. In Santa Cruz we had just bought a Buick Sky-Hawk as a second vehicle. We'd managed until now to find a location for the camper at the place where I ended my daily walking, but it was clear that it would be totally impractical to do that each day for the next eighteen months. Instead, we decided to locate the camper at one spot for about a week at a time. Alex would then use the car to shuttle Buck and me to and from the points on our itinerary that, according to his plan, would keep us on schedule.

Alex had designed a computer program that provided a detailed description of the entire route from San Francisco to New York. He had recorded in the computer's memory all the localities through which I would walk and the distances between them. He had also included details of the terrain, which he had gleaned from topographic maps and information he'd obtained from chambers of commerce and tourist guides. Every morning Alex would punch into the computer my actual location and, after a few seconds, the computer would print out a plan for the day. Alex would then show me on a map what the itinerary looked like, and from that we decided which roads and how many miles Buck and I would be walking. Most of the time this worked. Further, when circumstances like speaking engagements or illness put us behind schedule, Alex would make a few entries into the computer and the entire plan would automatically be modified.

Right now one of those engagements was about to throw us off course. We drove down the east side of Madonna Mountain (which I would come back to and walk that afternoon), and Alex dropped me off at the school. Some 250 children from kindergarten through the sixth grade were moving about trying to get comfortable on the floor of the gymnasium. I was introduced, and with no preparation began my first public speech of the trip.

"How many of you walk to school?" I asked the children. A few hands went up. This was a country school, so most youngsters came by bus. "How many of you have walked at least two miles?" More hands went into the air and some kids looked at each other and giggled. "Five miles?" Most hands went down. "Ten miles?" There was one hand left up, from a tot who I suspected had not studied measurements yet. "Well," I told them, "I have walked from San Francisco—I pointed on the large map of the United States that had been set up—"to the top of Hecker Pass." They knew where that was. "That is a distance of 125 miles and I have 3,775 miles to go, because I am walking from San Francisco to New York."

"On your feet?" came a spontaneous question.

"Yes, on my feet, and my dog Bucky is, too."

I got plenty of questions from those kids. "Where's Bucky?"

and "Does he get thirsty?" "Do you get blisters?" "Do you get hungry?" "How do you eat?" "Where do you sleep?"

Hands shot up, stretching and waving vigorously in each child's eagerness to be called on first. But one towheaded youngster sat just looking at me with wide blue eyes and a sweet shy smile. He didn't have to raise his hand; he had a question, and it was clearly written on his face. I pointed to him. "You, there." Quickly he closed his eyes, pursed his lips, sealing them shut, and shook his head. He had a question but he surely didn't want to ask it. "Yes, you have a question; it's okay, what is it?" I gently persisted. He clapped both hands over his mouth and pressed them hard to keep the question from escaping. "No, no," his wide eyes said as he shook his head again.

"It's really okay to ask anything," I repeated.

Finally he let his hands slide from his mouth, ducking his head and giving me a sidelong glance. I could barely hear him when he whispered "How do you go to the bathroom?"

Some of the children started to laugh, but then shifted their attention to hear how I'd answer. He was their voice; they'd all wondered. So I told them. "In San Francisco there are gas stations, cafés, and plenty of other public places where you can stop. Along the coast those places are separated by miles, and you have to plan ahead. In the forests or in the desert there are no convenient places to stop, but there's nobody out there either. Have you ever been in the woods?" He nodded. "So now you know. What do you do in the woods?" He ducked his head and smiled shyly again, but now he looked pleased.

Then one smart young lady, sitting in the back row, asked the question that would follow me for 3,900 miles: "Why are you doing it?"

Sure, there have been hundreds of questions, questions asked in this school and the hundreds of others that I visited across the country. And of course there were lots and lots of questions about Bucky—he was their hero—but the children also always asked "Why?" and I always told them what I told adults. There was no need to change or simplify the truth because they were children.

"Have you ever dropped a pebble in a lake or a puddle?" I asked, and they all had. (It seems that all children have, even in Death Valley, where there is no water.) "Then you have seen the ripples that you created that way. You've watched them move across the water farther and farther, until they reach the other side. But if the water surface is too large, you may not have been able to see them travel all the way across. Maybe the ripples were too small to see, but the energy from them was still there to reach the other side. The same is true for everything you do every single day. All our actions, all our attitudes, create ripples that reach others. You create ripples in your school, your neighborhood, your country, and even the world. A smile in the morning to your mom is more likely to make her smile than frown, and in that way ripples of happiness are started by you."

They understood, and like other children we visited along the way, they showed it in the letters they sent to Bucky and me, and in the hastily scribbled notes they passed to me as they filed out of the gym. That day a piece of red construction paper, carefully folded into a tiny envelope, was pressed into my hand. When I unfolded it, I read, "I love you, too." At the exit a girl moved close to me and slipped her hand into mine. Her name was Maria, and she was twelve, she told me. "I want to do something, too," she said. "I'm going to be a nurse."

Giving her hand a squeeze, I said, "What a neat idea!" And received the gift of her smile in return.

Before I left, I gave the children an address in Santa Rosa where the mail would be forwarded so that they could write to me. Several days after leaving Gilroy, I received a lavender envelope covered with red crayon hearts. "We want to do something to help you," the letter said. It was signed by Carol and Laurie, both seven years old. These young ladies had pooled their money and had taped six pennies to the letter. I wrote them back: "Thank you for your very special letter. Alex and I were very moved by your love. We wanted you to know we talked this over and decided to invest your money in a bone for Bucky. We love you."

There are lots of ways to make ripples.

Between Gilroy and the next town, Los Banos, fifty miles ahead, lies Highway 152, otherwise known as Blood Alley. I was told all about Blood Alley when I stopped for a cup of coffee before hitting the road again. Jerry, the owner of the coffee shop, stood by the counter. He had perfected the technique of flipping a cup from its saucer into the air and catching it in place. "What's the road ahead like?" I asked.

"It's called Blood Alley. That give you some idea?"

"How'd it get that name?"

"Trucks barrel through making up time. And the fog gets so thick can't see your hand in front of your face. It doesn't stop the truckers. They know the road and expect that everybody else does, too. Those rigs are powerful, and when someone tries to pull out in front of them, they sometimes can't stop in time—too much weight pushing them along. Average of two to five people get killed there every week." He turned away to start another pot of coffee. "How come you ask?"

"I'm walking that road."

"You'd better find another." He went down the counter, topping up coffee cups, then walked to a stand of packaged dry fruit, brought back a handful of packets, and set them down in front of me. "Here. Something for the road."

I didn't have enough pockets for all the fruit, but I crammed them in. "It looks like I have enough to take me to Oklahoma," I said. Then Buck and I resumed our walking.

Highway 152 is actually a narrow two-lane thoroughfare that connects three main arteries, State Highways 9 and 101 and Interstate 5. These link the major California produce areas—the San Joaquin and the Imperial valleys—with the rest of the state and the nation. Traffic on 152 is always intense.

This day's itinerary would take us on the long, dangerous stretch over Pacheco Pass, a cut through the Diablo Mountain Range, before we descended to the San Luis Reservoir. The next stop would be Los Banos, where I was looking forward to speaking with students in the elementary schools.

Day and night, bumper to bumper, two-trailer trucks roar through the pass at accelerated speeds, making up time on overdue delivery routes. As Jerry had warned, the dense fog that normally clogs the pass doesn't slow the drivers down one bit. Many a trucker barrels through at breakneck speed, miscalculates the distance and the responses of other drivers, then slams on the brakes too late. Out of control, they careen to a dizzying stop, truck jackknifed across the road, jamming traffic from either side. This stretch of Highway 152 is a death trap.

The road climbed straight as an arrow, and way up ahead it narrowed and disappeared into fog. There were no guardrails here to protect us from a fall, so we walked in the gravel, balancing precariously on the edge of the shoulder, which dropped down an embankment while elevating us high above the muddy roadside gutters. Empty cans and jagged glass from broken bottles were strewn among the rocks and weeds and would make a fall more hazardous should we be thrown into the ditch. Winds burst sporadically across the road, catching us off guard, slamming us with such force that I spent a lot of time crouching in order to be closer to the ground, all the while coaxing Buck to stay just behind me. Trucks rumbled down the slope, creating a wild turbulence that threatened to spin us around and topple us off the road, so every few feet I crouched myself into a ball, hugging tight to my cramping knees until the trucks passed. Sometimes I crawled on my knees.

Death lay all around us. We watched as a bird was swept into those turbulent cross currents of air and was slammed against the metal body of a hurtling truck, then tossed lifeless onto the side of the road. Hundreds of barn owls and hawks lay dead there. Some, badly stunned, were still flapping their wings helplessly, but would never rise again.

Gradually the afternoon sun began to settle into the Pacific behind us, filling the sky with a diminishing orange glow. Already lights were beginning to gleam in sheltered farmhouses cradled in the valley below. Thin trails of smoke curled from the chimneys of those warm and cozy-looking homes, where I imagined families gathering around the kitchen table. My teeth chattered and I trembled, longing for the secure warmth of our Santa Rosa home.

The wind carried a cutting dampness of fog, and the constant stirring of the air chilled me even more. I should have worn heavier clothing, but there was nothing to do about that now. I ducked again just in time. Another truck roared by with a velocity that spun me around. Up ahead I saw a string of them barreling down on us. I ducked down, crouching again, holding tight to my legs and hips, tucking my face down deep between my knees. Gravel spun like bullets from the tires and stung like gunshot, but there wasn't a whimper out of Buck. He knew what we were up against. "Stay, Buck. Steady, boy." I held his leash slack on the ground behind me. I used it as a guide for him to follow and to let him know I was with him all the way. I kept him behind me this way, unwilling to hook him onto his leash, because he wasn't used to being on a leash, and I couldn't be sure he wouldn't bolt, dragging us both under the tires of those heavy, fully loaded rigs. "That's it, stay behind me. Good Buck." Inch by inch I talked us up the road.

It took us three terrifying hours to cover the last six miles, but we finally crested the pass at 1,368 feet, where the gap cut through the hills, and there we were protected on both sides from the raw bitter wind. Drained, I dropped to the ground and closed my eyes, slumping against the jagged rocks. The trucks never let up. They continued to thunder through the cut in the hill. I was emotionally and physically exhausted. Buck dropped down beside me, wriggled his muzzle into my limp hand for solace, then rested his head on my thigh. I slung my tired arm over his shoulder. He looked up at me with his gentle brown eyes steeped in trust. "Between you and me," I confided, "I sure hope we don't have many more like that. That's one cruel place."

It was just as well that neither Buck nor I had any way of knowing that Blood Alley was only preparation for the trials that lay ahead.

The next day, walking down the eastern slope of Pacheco Pass was a breeze. By the time I reached Los Banos, the easier road had put us almost two days ahead of Alex's plan, so I walked from the highway to the schools where I had been invited to speak. I was coming away from the Los Banos Elementary School on that sunny, sweet-smelling day and thought I was alone when I heard, "Hi, there. Nice day for a walk." It was mid-January, but already California valley greens were flourishing in the fields, although not quite high enough to conceal someone from my view. I looked up. High in the branches of a tree, almost hidden among the leaves, a man stood in a cherry-picker basket, a buzz saw in his hands and a pile of branches beneath him on the ground.

"Hello," I called up to him.

"It's a beautiful day," he said, grinning. "Where you headed?"

A bit jauntily I threw it back to him—"New York"—and waited for his reaction.

He was willing to catch my humor, and with mock exaggeration he considered my response, then, tipping an imaginary hat, he pushed a button and glided smoothly to the ground. While standing in the basket, he looked at me with an expression that said he knew I was putting him on.

He cocked his head and asked, "You're going where?"

"New York," I said. "I left San Francisco on the fourth and I've come this far, 150 miles."

"Then why aren't you on the highway? You're going north."

"I just came from the school down the road."

He studied me, then asked, "You serious?"

"Sure." He rested the saw on his hip, thought about that a bit, and then threw me the test: "Why?"

"To see my country," I began. "To talk with young people. To encourage them to have their dreams. None of us has trouble with that, but we do seem to have trouble taking the first step toward making them come true." He was listening, so I continued. "I want to encourage youngsters to think about living their lives in a way that matters." It was not completely clear, but I could sense he understood.

To my surprise, I saw his eyes fill with tears, and a single one slid down his cheek.

"You know, I've had thoughts like that," he said. "I've wanted to do something like that, too. But you want to know what I've done?" His voice was tinged with self-contempt. He waited to see if I would really listen, and then went on. "For twenty-seven years I was a drug addict and an alcoholic. I gave it up. But that's what I've done." He said it as though that was the sum of his life. And as incredible as it was, it seemed at that moment the most natural thing in the world to be having this intimate conversation with this stranger on this road. "For twenty-seven years I wasted my life," he repeated, stuck in the sadness of it.

"Look," I said, "you've had an experience I haven't had. I don't know what it's like to be a drug addict or an alcoholic. It's probably not the best way to spend twenty-seven years. But you know what it's like, you've been there, it's real for you.

And not only that—you know the way out, because you've done that, too. So why not talk to others about it?" I asked.

He glanced up at me quickly, then studied his palms for a while, black from the dust in the trees. And then he shared his dream with me.

"I've thought about going to the high school and trying to reach the kids there. I'd tell them what it's really like. If they knew, they'd never get started."

"When are you going to do that?"

"Do you think they'd listen to me?"

"We all have something to say. It's up to us to decide if we want to say it."

It was over as quickly as it had started. His face was relaxed and happy. He knew what he was going to do. He offered me his hand and I took it, and we stood like that: I in the road, he in the cherrypicker. Then without another word I turned and headed down the road again. He pushed the button and I heard the motor carrying him into the trees. Another half mile and I turned to look back.

He was waving and so was I.

A short distance down that same mud-rutted country road an old farm truck rattled to a stop beside me. The burly, stubble-chinned driver in Big Ben coveralls called out, "Where you goin'?"

He intruded into my thoughts, which were still with the man in the trees, so I made it short. "Walking."

"Where?" he persisted dully. This man didn't seem too sharp—it looked like he wanted a pickup, and that's it.

"To the highway."

"Well, get in, I'm goin' that way. Put the dog in back."

"No, I said I was walking, so that's what I'm going to do." Then as an afterthought I called back to him, "But thanks, anyway."

He put the truck in gear and moved it forward at my pace, "Awwww, come on. No one will know."

I turned around. "That may be, but I would." And I lifted my hand in a gesture to let him know that the conversation was over.

In another twenty minutes I was back on Highway 152, heading east at a fast clip. Suddenly I was aroused by the drone of an engine. When I turned to look up, I noted with alarm a crop duster coming in for a pass over the chard field on my left. He skimmed the surface of the crop and discharged a load of poisonous yellow dust over the greens. The wind was blowing in our direction, swirling billowing clouds of noxious contaminant across our path. I grabbed a scarf and held it over my nose. "Let's get out of here," I yelled over my shoulder to Buck, and ran at top speed, backtracking the five miles into town. On that day we did not make much headway.

The following day, we crossed Interstate 5, that great artery running north and south, the length of California, through the bountiful, crop-yielding San Joaquin Valley. Migrant workers in colorful cotton shirts were already working in the fields. Nearby, teetering stacks of cardboard cartons waited to be filled with compact heads of cabbage.

In general I stayed off the interstates. It's illegal to walk them, for one thing, and highways and back roads are invariably more interesting. It was early morning, and the sun had not yet burned through the fog that hung heavy over the valley. I could scarcely see ten feet ahead. Pulling the hood of my navy blue zippered sweat jacket up over my head, I tightened the drawstrings around my face and tied them under my chin. No matter how many weather reports I listened to on the R.V. radio or read in the news, I still didn't seem to have the hang of dressing perfectly for the road. Sometimes I wore my quilted jacket, but then the sun would almost surely come shining through the fog and beat down on us, and then

I'd regret it. I envied Buck's simplicity. Rain or shine, he could get by with only a collar (although there was his "wolf" costume in case of emergency). Today I'd dressed too lightly again, so I jammed my hands deeper into the shallow pockets of my lightweight sweatpants and hunched my shoulders to protect myself from the bone-chilling cold. Buck trotted at my side, head down. He was cold, too. But I knew him. If he got too cold, he'd trot for a long while, stirring up body heat. Unlike me, there seemed no limit to the miles he could add that way. The grass on the side of the road was dense and wet, matting the hair on his belly, so we walked in the gravel on the slant of the shoulder, in the direction of Highway 99. Here a wide median strip divided the road, and down deep in the center I saw a trough, a shallow cement drainage ditch. "Come on, Buck. That's a better place to walk." Buck, always willing to listen to a good idea, loped along and we got down in the vee, appreciating its protection. Suddenly a car pulled to a stop at the side of the road off to my right and a highway patrolman, a sergeant, threw open his door and jumped out.

"What the _____ are you doing out there?" he bellowed.

I turned around, startled by his aggression. He was glaring at me, waiting for an answer.

"Why, I'm walking." It seemed reasonable to me. Then, to be sure he really understood, I added, "It's more protected in here."

"Get over here," he ordered, jabbing his finger in front of his feet.

Buck and I climbed up the wet grassy slope out of the vee, waited for a break in the traffic, and then crossed over the road to face the officer, although I instinctively kept a cautious distance from him. Buck stood beside me, a low, slow growl emanating from his throat. I knew Buck well enough to be sure that he was only making noises, not even considering more aggressive behavior. I wrapped his leather leash tightly around my fingers as he strained forward, his eyes fixed on the sergeant. I patted his shoulder reassuringly and murmured, "It's okay, Buck," to let him know that I was in control.

"What are you doing out here?" the officer demanded, so belligerently that I began to wonder if there was some law I inadvertently was transgressing. But still I didn't worry. It would be all right—wouldn't it?

"I was walking," I explained, choosing simplicity in order to clear things up quickly. "On that side of the highway." I turned and pointed. "Facing the traffic. It's cold, so we got down in the vee for protection." Apparently he had misjudged me, I thought, and like the police in Pacifica he would soon understand.

It became clear, however, that he meant to intimidate me. "What the _____ do you mean you were walking?" he snapped. "Where are you going?" I was stunned, but my mind strained to comprehend. How do I get through to this guy? I wondered.

"Chowchilla," I said, naming a town about eighteen miles away.

He stood hands on his hips, leaning forward at the waist, his lips curled. "Chowchilla?" He made it sound foul, but at that moment a second patrol car pulled up behind him. Thank goodness, I thought, now we'll get to the bottom of this. The second officer came up behind the sergeant, and now they both stared down at me. What could possibly be going on? I hadn't done anything wrong. I couldn't be accused of something I didn't do, could I? But obviously he wanted to find me guilty of something—I didn't know what or why.

"Don't you know it's illegal for you to be out here?" the sergeant snarled.

"No, I do not. I know it's illegal to walk freeways. This is not a freeway."

"You have identification?"

"Surely." I reached for my wallet, and the second officer's hand moved toward his gun. And then I remembered something in my pocket that might set things straight, an article I had saved from the Los Banos paper. So I pulled it out and smoothed out the creases. "Are you from Los Banos?" I asked the sergeant. He wouldn't answer. He'd ask the questions, not answer them. I turned to the second officer. "Are you?" He nodded slightly. "Then you may have seen this." I held up the front page of the *Los Banos Enterprise.* "Tom Wright, the editor, wrote this about me. Your mayor has welcomed me and I have spoken in your schools. I don't know what's happening here, but if you call either of those men they'll verify who I am and what I'm doing."

"You can't walk this road," the sergeant warned.

"I've got to walk this road to get off it. If it's illegal, I'll find out, and if that's true, I'll find another route."

"Like what?"

"Highway 99."

"I'm telling you it's illegal, and if I see you do it, I'll pull you in." It was subtle but I could tell he was backing off.

"And if I'm late," I challenged, meeting his threat, "my husband—"

"Your husband? Where is he?"

"In Chowchilla, expecting me. If I'm late, he'll be looking for me." And believe it, I took real comfort in knowing that was true.

But the sergeant was not ready to give up. "You get smart with me," he said, "and I'll throw you someplace he'll never find you." And I believed if pushed too far, he would have done it. Then: "But I'm giving you another chance."

All I wanted was to get out of there; he was too dangerous. I nodded and started to cross the road.

He screamed like a maniac, "What the ____ are you doing?"

"I'm crossing, to walk toward the traffic."

He jabbed his finger at the grass so vigorously that I felt he'd drive a hole into it. His face turned purple and veins throbbed on his neck. "I told you not to move from the grass. You do as you're told, and remember," he threatened, "I'll be watching for you."

And with that he stalked to his car, got in, slammed the

door, and spun into the road, leaving me in the dust. I stood there on the road shaking violently, but not from the cold. Oh, no. What seethed through my veins was rage, pure white-hot indignation. The second officer stayed a few more moments, looking at me lamely. He actually looked apologetic, yet he hadn't dared to stand up against his bullying fellow officer. What was he afraid of? He wanted to say something to me but seemed too fearful to speak up. He gave a brief nod and left also.

I was irate, shaken, and confounded. And I carried these feelings out on the road with me. For months, every time I thought about it I'd feel again the fury, fear, and confusion stirred up by that officer's provocation.

What had he intended? I still didn't know, just as I will never know or understand the passivity of the other officer. The sergeant had reached out and touched me, all right, but with a need to demean and diminish. He'd created his own ripples—ripples of wavelike force. For sure they were not the kind of ripples I had talked to the children about. But he had not won. I was as convinced as ever, as unshaken in my belief, that the force of those violent waves could be dissipated by the answering force of decency.

Though I'd trained strenuously in preparation for our journey, I hadn't included Buck in the training, thinking that he and I would have plenty of time to handle his training on the road.

Until the day we left, Buck had spent his life indoors as a dog of leisure, or—so he liked to think—a lapdog (although admittedly a rather large one). Every day, at home, Buck went for a twenty-minute early morning stroll, patrolling the boundaries of our property, which consisted of an acre of land in the Sonoma County's Valley of the Moon, just north of San Francisco.

In between those rounds, he spent his days lounging around

the house, sometimes with Alex, sometimes with me, but always the loyal companion of whoever was preparing food in the kitchen. Buck was a lazy dog—not fat, just lazy—and it seemed that he enjoyed it that way.

At home he had learned to follow commands like "Wait." When we came to an intersection, for example, he stood on the curb until I caught up with him and then we crossed together. He was reliable about it. He'd "sit" like a good dog when I stopped to ask directions, more, I think, for the attention he got than from good manners. "Your dog minds so well," people would say while patting him on the head. At those times Buck seemed to grin with pleasure. I could count on him to follow these commands, with one exception: when Buck saw a cat, he remembered nothing. As a result, some of his most painful and permanent lessons came from the experience of the road.

Buck acted as though our cross-country jaunt was taken purely for the fun of it, and while it's true that we made it a lot of fun, there also were times when we simply had to be respectful of existing conditions. Sometimes we would sit together, side by side, and I'd tell him about the mountains or the valleys. While he may not have understood all the words I used, he certainly felt the communication. We were good friends. Still I had to learn to be a better friend to Buck by making him more obedient to commands. Because the road would test him in ways I had never dreamed of.

We had now been walking together for three weeks. South of Fresno, Buck and I walked a road that divided fields of vines strung up on poles and wire, vines bearing grapes that later would be dried into raisins. The old wooden farmhouses were few and far between and produce traffic flowed in both directions.

Buck ran ahead as usual, checking out everything of interest to him, which was a lot, and looking over his shoulder from time to time to make sure I was following. He stopped frequently to leave his scent, never a problem for him here because the irrigation canals provided him with a constant source of replenishing liquid. Even at the end of January, California valleys can be hot, and Buck took advantage of those canals not only to quench his thirst but to cool his body. At home Buck had a positive hatred for water; he was always one to avoid a bath. His holding capacity was sometimes stretched to the limit when he refused to venture into the rain to find relief. But now he enthusiastically flopped his body into any puddle he could find and would lie there cooling off while lapping up his fill. It didn't bother Buck if the water was muddy; it quenched his thirst and cooled his ribs and that's what mattered to him.

On this particular day, as Buck and I strolled along, I was thinking about my fifty-third birthday. It was only a week away, and the first of two I would celebrate on the road. It would surely be a happy day because my sons were coming down to join us. I was getting farther from home and I missed them.

Suddenly from the corner of my eye I saw a cat streak by, with Buck tearing after it. They skidded and disappeared behind a wood-enclosed water tower. I knew the cat was safe from Buck; cats always were. I heard Buck barking and I could picture him standing as usual, front paws against a tree, looking into the branches at the cat, who probably was languorously cleaning itself while resting on a limb just out of reach. I'd seen that scene so many times that I didn't think to stop. I kept walking down the road, confident that Buck would follow. Soon he'd whip up behind me and with his nose give my hand a nudge, his way of letting me know he'd returned.

But an eighth of a mile down the road I became aware that Buck had not followed, so I turned around. To my surprise I didn't see him, so I called, "Buck, Bucky, where are you?" He ran out from behind the water tower and saw me, so I turned and continued walking, certain now that he would join me.

But a few minutes later I looked again to make sure. He was nowhere in sight. Uneasy, I stopped and called again, louder, "Buck, hey, Buck, c'mon, Buck!" I waited and was greatly relieved when again Buck dashed out from behind the tower. "C'mon, Buck, get serious; you won't get him this time, either," I mockingly called to him. But in a more insistent voice, I yelled, "Let's go!" and to emphasize my point I turned abruptly and walked on. But not for long. After a shorter distance this time I turned yet again to make sure he was following. He wasn't.

I'd had it. "Buck," I demanded, "get here. Right now!" Buck darted out from behind the tower and started after me. "That's better." Then he stopped. Inexplicably he ran into the middle of the road, looked one way and then the other, and suddenly at top speed, sped away from me. "Buck, what are you doing?" I shrieked. "No, Buck, this way." Too late, I watched as he disappeared farther and farther into the distance, running as though the devil were after him.

What had made him do that? I could only guess. Maybe my voice ricocheted, causing him to think I had called from that direction. At any rate he was off, gone, and I was frantic.

I started running after him, but after a mile I slowed down. I was out of breath and he was nowhere in sight. Until then I'd thought that Buck would discover his mistake, fully expecting to see him running back to join me. But he hadn't. I began to get worried. Where was he? Why had he gone the wrong direction? When I last saw him, he was running in the road. He'd be killed, or he'd get lost. Who knew where he'd stop?

I ran to the driveway of the nearest house, climbed to the porch, and rapped on the door. No one answered. I tried again but still got no answer, so I ran to the road and started again in the direction I'd seen him going. Now another worry crept into my head. While I was on that porch I had been concealed by a hedge. If Buck had come running back, he could have gone right past and not seen me. We could be looking for each other in different directions now. I had to decide, so I continued in the direction I'd been going, toward where he had disappeared.

Way up ahead, I saw two children playing in a dusty yard. They were swinging on a tire hanging by a rope from a giant tree. Hope sprang into my heart. Maybe their parents were home and would give me a ride so that I could cover the road faster. I ran into the yard, but in my excitement I talked too fast and startled them. Keeping my eye on the road, I tried to sound calm. "Have you seen a big red dog go by this way?" They shook their heads. Their eyes were large. "Is your mother home?" Again they shook their heads. "Your father?" No. "Anybody?" Nobody was home. "Okay, thanks," I called over my shoulder, hoping I hadn't upset them too much.

Far down the road, I saw a truck pull into a driveway and a person get out and enter the house. I ran the distance to the door and rapped loudly. No one answered. But I knew I'd seen someone enter. I went to a window, looking in on a kitchen, rapped on the pane with my knuckles, and waited again, facing the road in case Buck ran by. I had to find him. What if he had left the road altogether? I dared not think about it. I pressed my face to the glass. A cup of coffee, an open purse, and some keys rested on the table. Someone had been sitting there. Impatiently I took a coin from my pocket and rapped continuously. Then, in the dark of the house, I saw a figure walk toward the door. It opened very slowly, just a crack, and I saw the chain in place and the tip of a shoe blocking it from behind.

"What do you want?" a woman's voice demanded.

"I need help. My dog is lost." I rattled on, "I need a ride. Could you help me? Please?" I was desperate to find Buck— too desperate for her comfort.

"I saw you—you and the dog. What were you doing out there?" It sounded like an accusation.

That caught me up short. I hadn't expected suspicion, so I tried again to be convincing. I needed a ride from her. So much time had already gone by and dusk was coming on. It would make it more difficult to find him. But how crazy would it sound to tell her that I was walking to New York? I couldn't risk it. The chance of getting her cooperation already looked slim, but there was no one else around. It had to work, it just had to. So I tried again, carefully choosing my words, trying hard to sound believable.

"My dog and I were walking along the road," I started, deliberately slowing my speech hoping to sound calm and add to my credibility. "He got lost, I'm trying to find him. But"— and here my anxieties got the best of me again and I raced on—"he's running faster than I can walk and I don't know this area."

She watched with nervous confusion. "Please," I begged, and despair crept into my voice. "I see a truck there." I glanced over my shoulder at it. "Please," I pleaded, "can you give me a ride?" My eyes were brimming with tears. "I'll pay you," I added, hoping it would help. "I'll pay you for your time and the gas."

But still she held back. I couldn't control the tears that now rolled off my cheeks. "I don't want to lose him. I'm afraid he'll be lost forever." I'd reached the depths, it was hopeless. Buck was gone. I'd never find him.

I turned to leave, but heard her speak. "Wait," she said. I saw her struggling with her decision. Then: "I'll ask my husband." She wavered a moment. The quick glimmer of hope was gone. If she had to ask permission before she could help me, my chances were nonexistent. A man who requires that of his wife was not likely to say, "Go ahead and help a stranger." At the very best I would have to explain all over again and it would take more time while Buck was getting farther away. Maybe I should just get back on the road and continue on foot. But there were so many places to look, so many side roads he could take, so many fields to cross. I didn't know where to begin. Despondently I walked back to the road. Why, I wondered, by some miracle couldn't Alex come back for us early? We could look all night if we had to. We wouldn't stop. Buck is family.

And as though things were not already bad enough, it came to me then that Alex would come at the scheduled time to the place where he'd expect to find us, and we wouldn't be there, either of us. He'd search the road, but we were miles from where we should be. Should I turn back now or go on looking for Buck?

Then I heard the sound of an engine starting and saw the truck back up, turn around, and pull up beside me. "Get in. My husband's asleep. I'll take you." I could see by the expression on her face that she was taking a risk. "Where would you like to start?"

I didn't know. "Up there," I said, pointing in the direction he was last heading. We drove in silence, backtracking the roads Buck and I had walked, but there were endless deviations that could be explored. A steady stream of hedges, barns, fences, and roads leading in every direction flew past. He could be anywhere, hidden from view. We could even pass him without knowing it. I rolled down the window. My eyes searched everywhere, but it was foolish; we simply couldn't search everywhere.

After a long while she inquired, "How much farther would you like to go?" She was patient but her voice implied it wasn't reasonable that Buck could have traveled so far.

"I don't know, I really don't know. But I know I've got to find him." She was good enough not to say what was clearly on her mind; that it was not going to work. We were almost back to where we had started that morning. Buck would not have run that far back.

Off in the distance, we saw it together—a large pile of dirt pushed to the side of the road, with a bulldozer parked beside it. And at the very top of that high mound we saw something move. Could it be? Could it possibly be Buck? I hardly dared to think so, and we were still too far away. "It could be," she said thoughtfully as though reading my mind, with more hope that I dared express.

"It is, it is," I yelled, ready to grab the wheel. But she was ready and more calm than I: "I'm going past him. I'll make a U-turn and come back on his side of the road." It was practical—he wouldn't have to cross the road—but I could hardly sit in my seat while we passed him by, turned and came back. I saw him standing at the top of the hill, just standing up there, surveying the landscape as though deciding where to go next. His nose was raised, sniffing for a scent, a clue to lead him on. Almost before she pulled to a stop, my door was open and I jumped out. "Buck!" I yelled. Well, that dog just tore up the dirt getting down off that hill, and he ran to me, nearly knocking me over. Lifting his paws onto my chest, he licked my face with a scrubbing that almost took the skin off. But I didn't care. He and I were together again.

I made good my promise and offered to pay the woman. "Are you kidding?" she said, looking pleased that she'd decided to help me, after all. "Where can I take you?"

"Why not in front of your house?" And that's what she did.

It took Alex an hour to find us, and when he did, he was concerned. "What happened?"

"Just wait," I said, rolling my eyes. "Wait until I tell you. You won't believe it."

Well, I'd like to say that Buck never chased cats again, but it simply wouldn't be true. Buck continued to play that game, and it got him into lots more trouble. The best I can say for him is that he never again lingered so long, and he's never lost me again.

As it turned out, there were lots of things that happened along the way that I hadn't thought about in advance, including what Buck's actions could be when he encountered animals he'd never seen before. A few days later, when we were approaching Porterville, a town about forty miles north of

Bakersfield, Buck rounded a bend in the road and ran head-on into a herd of cows. It was then that I'd wished I had started his training earlier.

Buck was ahead of me, as usual, and I saw him stop dead in his tracks. He looked directly into the shaggy white faces of hundreds of milk cows, and they seemed as astonished to see Buck as he was to see them. Beside their bulk Buck looked like a mighty small dog indeed. The cows stopped chewing their cud, and those still lying on the ground stood slowly and clumsily, turning to face him. A few stepped forward and hung their heavy heads over the barbed-wire fence. Buck watched them a few moments and then to my alarm he stepped forward and dared to bark. I believe he was completely surprised when those animals pulled their heads back over the wire and quickly jostled away, their heavy udders jiggling beneath them.

Buck's ears lifted. This promised to be more fun then he'd counted upon. Without considering the consequences he ran forward repeating the challenge, and the herd galloped away.

Buck was in heaven. I could see it in his eyes. The game was on and he was ready to play. From a standstill, without a warning he jumped, easily clearing the wire fence, and landed gracefully in the pasture, ignoring my pleas to stop. Barking, he drove the herd deeper into the pasture. I was terrified that a farmer would come running and with some justification take aim with his rifle and bring Buck down. I was desperate to get him back. But Buck was having too much fun even to hear me. Nipping at the cows' hooves, he kept them on the move until he cried wolf once too often. Suddenly they slowed down, came to a lumbering halt, and slowly, one by one, turned around and began to advance on him.

The game was over. Buck backed up and barked, but it didn't sound quite so convincing. They kept coming. He backed up again and barked; they kept coming. The expression on Buck's face changed, the narrow furrow on his brow clearly showing his perplexity. He decided to get out of there fast, but he hadn't allowed time or space to make his leap safely. He tried, but didn't clear the wire fence. His heavy black collar caught on the barbs and Buck was hooked, trapped, hanging helplessly by the throat as the cows moved in on him.

I didn't know what those cows would do. Would they ram him with their heads? Throw him to the ground and trample him to death with their hooves? I had to do something. But I was separated from him by a wide drainage canal, water rushing through it with such force that anything would be washed away. Still I had to save him and I started wading into the water, already thinking about how I would lift nearly one hundred pounds of dead weight off the wire.

But Buck wasn't waiting around to find out what might happen next. His eyes rolled in the direction of the moving herd. He jerked his muscles convulsively, contracting them violently, bouncing his body against the brutal barbs, and I watched with horror as the cruel metal points punctured his beautiful sleek hide. He kept at it until he managed to throw himself off the fence right at the feet of the cows. Now he had no time left. He made a painful escape, scraping himself through the lower wire rungs, scoring ugly bloody grooves deep in the flesh of his rump.

He jumped into the canal, swam across it with the current, dragged himself up the bank, and dropped at my feet. I put my arms around my soggy dog. I knew I hadn't been fair to him. I hadn't prepared him for the road as well as I'd prepared myself. His training was long overdue.

From that point on we both learned to mind his manners. If I said no, it was no—without question. He had crossed the line from a pet to a companion, one I could depend upon to obey.

FOUR

•••••••••••••••••••••••••••••••••••••••

Should We Stop Walking?

On my fifty-third birthday, February 4, my two sons and their families drove the 220 miles from their homes south of San Francisco to Kingsburg, south of Fresno, to celebrate the day with us. They later told me that while making the five-hour trip, watching the landscape flash by, the hills, the pastures, the fields, the valleys, driving on and on, they kept repeating among themselves, "Mom walked this!"

It was wonderful to see them after a month's separation and to share some adventures from the first miles. We picnicked with the ducks on the bank of the Kings River and had trouble keeping the birthday candles lighted while I made a silent wish. Now that it's over, I can share my wish—that we'd all be well and reunited at the end of the eighteen-month journey. When it came time for them to leave, Gary said pensively, "Mom, it's a long drive from San Francisco. And it's going to be longer and longer." He was saying good-bye. With a smile to cover the poignancy of the moment, I teased him gently, "Gary, if I can walk it, you can drive it." Anyway, it hurt to know it would be a long time before I saw them again.

To me the weekend had been more than a birthday celebration; it was also the day I realized the completion of my sons' emancipation from me, and of mine from them. Although they promised that they'd try to fly in for a midcontinent reunion, I didn't really believe it would be possible; and a seventeen-month separation was a long time.

From the very beginning of their lives I had wanted them to be as confident, capable, and caring as possible. I didn't want to transfer to them my own prejudices, my own fears, my own judgments. I didn't want to repeat empty words to them, things I'd been told and wasn't sure of myself. I wanted to pass along those things that I really came to know, and I realized that I knew little. I wanted them to experience life for themselves, and I gave them opportunities to do that. This included getting them acquainted with what nature has given us to observe. We'd visit the park close to home, walk the woods, and look for new discoveries.

They were very young when I knew I could trust them to take their poles and go by themselves to fish out on the pier. One day they watched a fisherman bring in a shark from the bay and throw it on the pier to die. It lay there flopping about, suffocating, and they couldn't bear it. When I picked them up, they wanted to bring the shark home. We did. The shark was already languid. I didn't give it much hope, but still I filled the bathtub, and trying to simulate seawater, I poured table salt into it. I learned later that this mix doesn't come close to approximating seawater, but it was worth a try. The three-foot shark did not survive, but she gave birth to six baby sharks before she died, and we called the Steinhart Aquarium, which agreed to take the babies.

Another day I left Guy and Gary at the children's museum while I went to the library. When I came back, I spotted them running over the hill toward me, and when they were closer,

I saw that Gary had a snake in his hand, holding it high so that I could see it.

"Look, Mom," he said, "look what I got. I only paid ten cents for it." It was a garter snake. Some enterprising youngster had found it on the hill and sold it to Gary. He was excited, though he turned his arm over and said, "Look, it bit me."

I knew the bite was harmless, but I preferred having it checked. So, not thinking, I said, "Let your brother hold it while we have that looked at." And he did. Whereupon the snake struck again, this time biting Guy. Now they both had to be checked. "Just put the snake in the back seat of the car," I said, and we went back to the museum, where the bites were cleansed and the curator confirmed that the snake was indeed harmless.

When we came back to the car, the snake had disappeared. We looked under the seats, behind the seats, between the seats, but still we couldn't find the snake. I was late for my remaining errands so I told the boys we had to go, but remembered thinking to myself, We'll be driving in rush-hour traffic and I don't want that thing to surprise me.

I left them at the house to take their showers and went to shop at the grocery store, completely forgetting about the snake. When I opened the back door to put my groceries in the car, the snake dropped out and slithered under the car. I was determined to protect Gary's investment and bring it back home. Both the boys had shown so much interest and excitement about it. So I bent to look under the car, and at that moment another car pulled up alongside of me and a young man got out. Seeing me on my knees looking under the car, he courteously asked, "Did you lose something?"

"Yes," I said, "I lost a snake." He was startled and looked at me with skepticism, but I was serious enough to be convincing. The man was exceptionally polite, yet it was impossible for him to hide his apprehension about looking for a snake, though he gallantly stayed to help me. Eventually we captured the snake and dropped it into a brown paper sack. Then, leaning back on the car and letting out a long sigh, he asked, "Tell me, do you always take that snake shopping with you?"

The snake lived with us for a few days in the basement before establishing freer residence in the garden.

I gave my boys credit for being responsible for their own well-being. Even when they acted irresponsibly, it didn't in any way reduce my trust in their ability to be accountable.

One day Guy came home with an idea that he had discussed with other high school students. He was sixteen at the time. They wanted to take their bicycles and ride from Denver, where we lived at the time, to San Francisco. I was no more shocked than he was later when I told him I would walk across America. I evaluated his capability to do it, as Alex would later do for me, and I concluded that he was responsible enough to handle what could happen on the roads, responsible not only for himself but for the other young people in the group. So he did it and gained a lot of experience about himself and the world he lives in.

With that kind of relationship, my children and I have always had tremendous respect for each other. They like to be with me and I with them, and since my marriage to Alex, they have managed to keep up their open communication with me, even if in the beginning they felt that I was no longer as available to them.

So I was aware that when I told them about the walk, they would be disappointed about the separation, yet at the same time, would support it and me with love.

When I took my first steps, I knew where I would also take the last. I wanted those last ones to be at the feet of Lady Liberty. I could have died on the road, I knew; it would simply have been another kind of last step. This was true for all of us—Buck and Alex as well. I could lose Bucky on the road, and while I took precautions to reduce that possibility, I couldn't wrap an impenetrable womb around us. I knew that we all would encounter many obstacles, that many times we'd face situations that would give us excellent reasons to quit. But I'd lived long enough to know that if I wanted to do something, the only way to do it was to do it, one step at a time, ten feet at a time or 82 miles at a time, whatever measurement worked. I knew that what gets in the way of doing the things we want to do are our justifications for not doing them, and that we are really good at finding such justifications. I'm too old, I'm too tired—all of those thoughts and more came up for me to accept or to laugh at. But I had trained myself to look for solutions. For sure, it's not always that easy. When we have disposed of our considerations, we still have to handle the obstacles, and my way of doing that is to consider them as challenges for which to find solutions.

Nine days after celebrating my birthday, on a gray and foggy California valley morning, that determination was tested to the extreme. Alex almost died.

My husband was born and educated in Belgium, in a family where money was scarce, but his mother intelligently managed the family budget, and a good portion of it was spent for sound nutrition. Even during World War II, when Alex was ten and Nazis invaded his country, that healthful diet continued. The mediocre rations and the expensive black-market offerings were complemented by products from Alex's grandma's little farm: eggs freshly collected from the barn, home-baked bread, milk still warm from the cow, and vegetables from the well-tended garden. In addition to that excellent start-up regime, Alex had practiced outdoor activities all his life: fourteen years hiking and camping with the Boy Scouts, which led to being an Eagle Scout; serious games of tennis, basketball, and soccer; several track disciplines; and intensive horseback riding. All in all, he was in much better physical shape than I was before I started my walk.

Because he had no history of health problems, Alex had developed an overly confident belief in his invulnerability. He was determined not to be sick, ever, and for the most part he had been successful. But five weeks into the journey, Alex made a suggestion that I now recall as unusual. He wanted to move for a day or two to a higher elevation. It would take us out of the valley fog, which he was finding depressing, while he reevaluated my itinerary. Everything we were doing so far was done by trial and error, so he requested the time to iron out some bugs in his planning. It was all right with me. I could use the time to redistribute our belongings inside the camper, putting our most used items in more convenient locations. So we moved to a campground on the banks of a river in peaceful, sunny Three Rivers, thirty miles away.

That first evening, after a shower, I was relaxing in the camper, Buck was asleep at my feet, and Alex was preparing dinner. We are both good cooks and enjoy preparing food, so we take turns fixing the meals. This night he abruptly left the mini-kitchen corner and headed toward the bathroom without a word. I came to a certain level of alertness and heard the sounds of vomiting. I knocked, but got no answer. Cautiously I tried the door. It was unlocked, so I pushed it open a crack and could not believe my eyes. The sink, the mirror, the floor, even the walls of the small bathroom, were splattered the brilliant red of blood.

When Alex saw me, he desperately tried to control his spasms, straightening his body as much as he could and lifting his head. After a few seconds that seemed to last a long time he uttered quietly, "It's nothing. I'm okay."

But I could not believe this. His face was as pale as white linen; he could barely stand, he was covered with blood. Still, he said he was okay. I helped him to the couch, where he gave up his resistance as I forced him to lie down. I told him to stay still while I called an ambulance. Protesting, he tried to sit up but fell back weakly. I rushed to the office of the campground and dialed the emergency number.

When I came back, Alex was outside leaning against the camper, violently vomiting more blood. Luckily, the paramedics arrived almost immediately. They put him on the ground, brought a stretcher, and transferred him to the ambulance. They would not allow me inside.

"What hospital are you taking him to?" I yelled as they jumped in after him.

"Miller Memorial. It's farther away but they have better facilities." The doors slammed. The vehicle was on its way.

I jumped in the car and followed them. The night was foggy and the ambulance was speeding like a racing car around the curves of the highway. I had problems keeping up with it. I didn't know the roads, and I had no idea where Miller Memorial was, so I had to take risks to stay close. I was desperately afraid I would lose them.

I arrived at the hospital in time to see them rush the stretcher inside the emergency room. When I entered, the medical team was already checking Alex's vital signs. His blood pressure was more than critical and his pulse had reached over 200 per minute. The doctor had ordered a blood transfusion. Alex had lost 50 percent of his normal blood content, the doctor told me. I was terrified. I could not imagine how that could have happened so fast.

Sure enough, this dramatic hour was only the culmination of three days of hidden illness. Later Alex admitted that the first symptoms had appeared in his feces earlier and that he had felt increasingly dizzy since then. The day before, when he asked me to drive—an unusual request—he had done so because he was afraid he would pass out. And when he had asked me to stop the car at the side of the road, it was to vomit blood, but he hadn't told me. It was "nothing," he said, "just an upset stomach."

It has taken me a while to understand what was happening in his mind at that time. Alex is brilliant. He holds three advanced university degrees and for more than thirty years, has been very successful in the computer industry, where he had exercised his logic extensively. How could he possibly pretend he was okay when everything indicated a very serious health condition? Why was he lying so blatantly? Well, as he told me later, he stubbornly refused to be sick. And he almost died because of that stubbornness.

The doctors would not let me spend the night in the intensive care unit, where Alex had been placed. They had started the blood transfusion, and, with a tube pushed into a nostril and down through the esophagus, they had pumped blood out of his stomach and were letting drops of iced water drip continuously on the ulcered blood vessel that had ruptured at the junction with the intestine. They hoped in that way to stop the hemorrhage. With instruments placed on the vital points of his body and connected to a computer, Alex's vital signs were monitored all night. It was too early to give any accurate prognosis of his survival, but the medical team estimated it at fifty-fifty. I had to leave—they insisted upon it—but I could call later in the night, they said, to check on his status. One doctor called a motel across the street and made a reservation for me. Numbly I left the hospital and checked in.

Alone in my room I pulled back the spread and sat down on the edge of the bed. From the window I could see the lights in the hospital. In one of those rooms Alex lay, I desperately wanted to let him know how close I was to him, longed to do the things that would ensure his survival. Instead, I felt helpless, separated, isolated at a time when closeness was more important than ever. And Buck—I hadn't had time to think about him. I had left him at the campground office in Three Rivers. Because the manager was aware of the emergency, she had accepted him without question. But ever since he had been lost in California he became frantic when we were separated. He surely must feel deserted, but there was nothing I could do. I had hoped to be with Alex, holding his hand, doing what needed to be done to comfort him. I had to leave Buck behind, and now, for the first time, all three of us were separated. I thought of going back to the hospital and finding a way into Alex's room, but I knew there was no way I could get past the nurses at the intensive-care desk. Instead, I made the first call to check in. "There's no change, Mrs. Hanuse; try to get some rest."

I left my telephone number after extracting a promise that I would be called if there was any change at all. I pulled back the covers and climbed in under the sheets with my clothes on, then sat up. Of course I wasn't sleepy. All I could think about was Alex and our journey.

We had met when we were both fifty, introduced by a mutual friend who said simply, "You'll probably like each other." And it was true.

We'd both been married before and had done much in life. What we really had in common was a keen interest in living, a willingness to explore life as an adventure and to take the risks of new experiences, but with a purpose, because we both are givers. We had discovered more satisfaction in supporting each other in doing the things in life that the other wanted to do than by competing. The disagreements that did come up between us were quickly repaired; having found that we would make up anyway, we shortened the time spent being angry to three seconds. It was a waste to spend time in any other way than in the harmony we normally had. A smile initiated by either of us was a signal to give up the disharmony. It didn't mean capitulation; we have too much respect for one another's independent thinking. It simply meant, let's not waste time when we can spend it on being happy.

When I first met Alex, it did not take me long to discover the depth of personality that lay behind the surface. Alex was knowledgeable about a multitude of subjects, discussing them easily, but what came shining through all that, and what makes Alex very special to me, is his compassion, his ability to feel and express emotion, his warm sensitivity—and that he's never lost the strings to his heart.

Our first date, a lunch, lasted four hours, and when we said good-bye I kissed him on the cheek. It surprised him but it was my way of telling him how much I appreciated him, his humanity, his concern for human beings.

The night took forever. Every hour on the hour, I called to check my husband's condition. At four in the morning Alex was in critical but stable condition. At seven he was adamantly demanding to leave the hospital. That was a signal I recognized: Alex would live! But I had to find a way, fast, around his stubborn nature and I could not see an easy route. Trekking across the country seemed easier! For sure I had no practical argument to convince him to stay in treatment. The doctors had tried to reason with him on that score. I did the same, but it was hopeless. Only under sedation could he be kept quiet, and that was not a long-term solution. I inquired about the type of treatment that Alex would receive at the hospital: basically rest and observation. The night-long transfusion had replaced the missing blood. The ulcer had stopped bleeding, but could reopen at any moment, so rest and constant attention were called for.

Could I provide rest and attention in our house in Santa Rosa? Sure, but could I get him to sit still for the rest and attention he so desperately needed? Neither one of us was very good at sitting still. Alex would be morally affected by that decision. He has always said that he would prefer death to physical confinement, and I was unwilling to gamble on how serious he was about this statement. Could he find rest in our camper? I came close to saying "Of course," but realized that I could not help Alex without his support. The question of whether to continue the trip or abort it had to be resolved. That's when I decided to talk to him.

I started with the bad news. Coffee would irritate the ulcer, the doctor had said, and Alex, like most Belgians, was accustomed to drinking cup after cup. Alcohol was also taboo, and Alex had lived many years in France, where a glass of wine with every meal is as deep a tradition as eating bread and butter. Would he be willing to give that up? And would he be conscious of his vulnerability and be willing to share with me all symptoms that might indicate bleeding?

Alex listened, and between the lines he understood that the completion of the walk was in the balance. "I'll make it to New York," he said, knowing that it implied cooperation on his part. We had come to the same decision. We would be prudent but we would go on. I made him promise that we would always try to be near a medical facility, sometimes a trick in the most remote regions. There would be, for both of us, more of life to taste by going on than by turning back. And we both knew now that if something happened to either of us, the other would find a way to complete the journey we had started together.

When we came back to the campground, where Bucky had been left alone in the office for eighteen hours, we found the place torn apart: not a drape had been spared; the furniture was upside down. A hurricane would not have done more damage. Someday it will be proven that dogs know when their master is in danger; Buck, I can tell, knew better than any of us that my husband's life hung, for one terrible evening, in the balance.

FIVE

···········•••••··•••••··•••··•••••··•

Crossing Death Valley

Three days of rest in the beautiful community of Three Rivers, southeast of Fresno, was all it took for Alex to feel ready to hit the road again. There, on the bank where three rivers join, the sun reflected brilliantly on the snow-covered mountains directly up the river canyon.

We met Trudy, a warm and loving local person who became one of our lasting transcontinental supporters. She invited us to speak at the Three Rivers School, and this made us well known, at least by the children, in that friendly town. "Hi, Alex" was a frequent greeting from smiling young faces when Alex felt well enough to go into town, and I'm sure their friendly regard did much to contribute to his speedy recovery. With some regret but with the intention to return someday, we left, with three days of walking to make up.

Every day was new, nothing routine about it except mundane things like brushing my teeth and pulling on my sweats in the morning. Every day Buck and I walked places we'd never walked before, always exploring new territories, always walking into the unknown. It took a while to get used to being left on the road with only a daily itinerary, a list of roads, streets, and maybe detours to guide us. When Alex drove off and left us alone on the side of the road, Buck and I watched until the car disappeared from view, and I always felt the desolate sadness of abandonment.

By the time we had walked 1,000 miles and were past the eastern border of Nevada, I would become somewhat used to being totally alone except for Buck. Fear doesn't ordinarily stop me. I see it as something distinct and separate from wanting to do something; I have lived long enough not to have fear be a barrier for me—at least it had been that way until I got to Old Kern Canyon Road.

But now, three hundred miles south of San Francisco, we turned east, at last. No more walking the wrong way. We left the desert heat of Bakersfield and entered the cool shade of Kern Canyon. Following the river, we climbed the canyon heading for the dense forest wilderness of Sequoia National Park, planning to cross the Sierra Nevada Mountains at Walker Pass. Of all the narrow roads we walked, this one was the skimpiest. Highway 178 hugs the rock canyon walls in tight convolutions. As a result, we often crossed over and pressed against the hillside rather than walk along the river's edge, since there was little foot room, and no traffic barricades to prevent a fall. Another hazard was that the twisted canyon walls blocked the sound of cars coming up from behind until they were almost upon us. We were constantly searching for rock wall crevices to squeeze into until the traffic passed.

Our itinerary that day took us beyond the point where the road divided. On our left it became a freeway. "Don't go to the left," Alex had advised. "Take the road to the right—the Old Kern Canyon Road." Right on target we came to the fork in the road, turned to the right, and entered the stillness of the forest. The sweet smell of sun-warmed pine needles filled the air, the wind rustled branches ever so gently, and soon we were swallowed into the total solitude of the woods. Buck ran through the brush and I heard him clearly: twigs snapped, branches cracked, and from time to time I heard him barking, a signal that he'd chased another squirrel into the safety of a tree.

After several hours of that, even Buck was tired, so he joined me, walking silently by my side. But, strangely, the sound of branches snapping and the crushing of leaves continued. The afternoon sun became lost in the tops of the trees. Shadows grew longer and silence deeper, and in the eerie atmosphere of the dusk my mind found it easy to rush to improbable images that stirred up childish fears. I felt it happening. I listened more closely to the noise of the woods; deep in the dark of the impenetrable forest the animals walked with us and I remembered the warnings of the schoolchildren.

"You're walking Old Kern Canyon?" they asked incredulously.

"Why not?"

"There're wild bear and boar in there."

In the safety of their classroom I scoffed, but with dusk my vulnerability gave way to fear. I let it happen; my imagination took over. The animals of the forest! Buck and I were no match for any one of them. I got rid of our remaining rations, throwing them into the bush so as not to have a lure and regretted my decision for having laid out a skimpy meal: surely they would come for more.

I was more willing to risk the freeway than to face the bear and boar. We had only a short distance left to rendezvous with Alex, and yet I turned abruptly and started back the other way. At least the road we'd covered was familiar. I walked fast, then faster, then trotted, the unknown darkness behind us pushing me ahead, and finally broke into a run as though the forest would grab and hold us. Fueled by fear, my panicking mind was in control, and though I knew I shouldn't, I was heading the wrong way.

When we reached the fork in the road, I felt relieved by its familiarity. Cars raced by on the freeway and we followed.

Soon my mind cooled and I realized what I had done. But what choices were there now: turn again and enter the forest? I wasn't willing. Yet Alex would be there right now looking for us.

He knew my normal pace and would determine how far we would have traveled and where we ought to be. Later he was to tell me he went back and forth, searching, thinking he'd made a mistake in his calculations. He went a mile too far in one direction, then the other. Panicked himself, he traveled many miles too far in both directions and didn't find us or any sign of us, nothing that would indicate what might have taken us from the road. He couldn't imagine what had happened. And he dared not to think the unthinkable (he, too, knew about the bear and boar). She cannot have taken the freeway, she would not have done that, his rational mind said. After much frantic searching he headed for the nearest town to get some help. He took the freeway, the fastest route, and there, on the side of the road, he found us, weary, cold, and going the wrong way.

In Old Kern Canyon Road I discovered that I was still only prepared to deal with fears that were familiar—logical fears of the road. In the forest I got a vivid view of how one's mind can defy logic, making the irrational seem real. There I learned the treachery of a mind out of control; and that mind was mine.

At long last, Buck and I crossed over the Sierra Nevada at Walker Pass, and we stood there awhile, looking out over a never-ending valley. Way off in the distance we could see the mountains called the Panamint Range. But stretching in front of us was the thin narrow ribbon of a road that wound its way down off the hillside and reached out into eternity across the empty valley floor. The landscape was dotted with chaparral, sagebrush, and cactus, but not a drop of water could be seen. This was hot, dry, arid country. Each day dawned with a brilliant radiant sun opening up the desert silence. By midday the scorching sun bore down on us, while during the night the temperature plunged to a brutal deathly cold.

We passed Inyokern, Ridgecrest, and Trona, and the road started climbing steadily. When we crested the range, we had a view of the basin where I knew the gates to Death Valley lay. Buck and I stood still, surveying the scene. The view before us was devastating. The road continued stretching like a long ribbon between the foothills of the Argus and Slate mountain ranges. I knew we had to walk it, but saw no other signs of life out there. Even so, I was not too apprehensive about the basin road. What I feared the most was the narrow passage that would bring me down to the valley. There the road slanted off toward a cliff and I knew that my fear of height, that creation of my mind, would again plague me, pulling at me, drawing me toward the edge, dragging me forever into a horrible measureless abyss. I was terrified to take this part of the walk but I was going to have to do it even if I had to clutch at the boulders, hang on to sagebrush, anything to prevent my going over the edge. But for the moment I sat down in a roadside gulley, which cradled and protected me so I could not be frightened by the sight of the plunge and could therefore let my mind roam free.

Suddenly I saw an animal—a roadrunner. He sped across the road and disappeared into the brush, but his brief appearance began to restore my sense of being at peace with myself and one with nature. I felt a bond of kinship with him; we had so many things in common. We were sharing the same environment, the same ranges and basins, the same road, the same rocks, the same horizon that we knew we could reach to discover another that we could also share.

My mind was exploring this universe that he and I are part of when my attention was drawn to a bee circling nearby. I had in my pocket a carton of juice. I opened it and poured a few drops into a cavity in a nearby rock. Sure enough, the bee accepted my invitation and started sipping our juice. I felt totally aligned in the simplicity of being out there with that bee and the roadrunner, and I noted that, in the midst of life's complications, we share a common ground with all creatures—every one of them.

If my mind could make the connection with the roadrunner, with the bee, making me know, with an essential knowing, that we can communicate, that we are one, so my mind can remove the fences and borders that we all construct between ourselves and other people. Perhaps my mind could even conquer the fears of my imaginings—falling off mountains, bridges, and all the other high places left ahead of me. With that barrier lifted at this moment, I was in absolute peace. Yes. Peace can result from the victory of our awareness over our mind.

Soon we were back on the road. Nightfall was coming and the abject loneliness of the road, the mountains, the surroundings grabbed me. It happened that a Phantom jet came screaming by at just a few feet above ground level, and I looked at that jet with its armored body and said to myself: There is a human being in there, there is somebody at least out here with me. But it didn't help a lot, because we could not talk with one another and I could not see him. His jet screamed up into the distance and I felt lonelier than ever.

Then I heard, and I saw behind me, way down the road, a truck that came rumbling up and went racing by me. Suddenly the driver slammed on the brakes, screeched to a stop, and backed up. His arm was hanging out the window. He looked out at me and said, "Can I give you a ride? Are you in trouble? Did you break down?"

"No."

"What are you doing out here?"

"I am walking."

"You are walking out here?" and he looked in both directions, and there was nothing.

"Yes, I am walking."

"Why?"

I told him that I was walking across America because I wanted to see my country. And he said, "Are you the lady I saw in the newspaper this morning?"

"Yes."

"My hat's off to you, lady. What can I do for you?"

"You just did it," I said.

His name is Jules, and what he did was stop and offer me support. We were able to share with each other. We hugged each other, and when he took off, I was feeling good being out there because another human being had offered me assistance.

The pickup truck disappeared around a curve in the road, and Buck stood and watched as though held by a dim memory. I could only imagine what he was remembering. If he could talk, perhaps he would have said:

"I am thinking of another truck and another person, the first person with whom I lived. He brought me to a strange house in a truck like that one. It was dark and late at night and he opened the truck door and called, 'C'mon, Butkus,' and I jumped out, eager to follow him. A lady stood waiting and we all entered the house. Very shortly he opened the door and went outside and I never saw him again. I heard the truck engine start and the sound of the tires pulling out of the driveway, and my heart leaped, for he was leaving without me. I jumped to my feet and ran to the window and watched the red taillights disappear into the night. 'It cannot be, he cannot be leaving without me.' I raced to the door, to the window, frantic to follow. 'It's a mistake, he cannot be doing this, he cannot leave me.' From my chest came the long mournful sounds I didn't recognize, but the voice was mine. I was abandoned. He was leaving me here and I was utterly wretched. I trembled and cried, a whine deep in my throat, as I raced from window to door desperately trying to find my way out of this strange home.

"The lady called me to her and for a minute I went. She knew my name and she put her arm around my shoulder, pulled me against her leg, and patted me. 'It's all right, Buck, you're going to be okay. He couldn't keep you, Butkus, but you will like it here.' Her voice was gentle and reassuring but my heart broke and I stayed there and trembled and I realized he wasn't coming back. Now when I watch that truck disappear into the curve, that distant, distant memory pulls at me. At first I want to run and catch up to the truck, but instead I stand and watch, and only the dimmest memory continues to pull at me.

"And the lady who is now my friend walks up beside me and puts her hand on my shoulder; she understands."

Death Valley. The very name conjures up harsh images of sun-bleached bones on a scorched and searing desert floor. Hawks wheeling monotonously overhead, in the white heat of the motionless sky, do not improve that image. Here you know you're dealing with a major force. The Panamint Range on the west and the Funeral Mountains on the east enclose the 140-mile-long desert with relentless heat and a scathing silence. Death Valley is a vast, demanding, and merciless host; names like Furnace Creek, Devil's Cornfield, and Funeral Peak tell its story. Out here, you are obliged to confront awesome conditions that, if you are foolish, can take your life.

Buck and I came into the desert in February. It was part of our overall plan that we would cross the valley before the heat made it totally impossible to do so. In summer temperatures soar to over 130 degrees. Only an occasional tourist drives in there—and then only by accident. Already it was hot as Hades, and while the temperature at night dips dramatically, during the day it never cools.

I had dressed too warmly as usual, wearing a polo shirt and light sweatpants. We'd planned on taking two weeks to cross the valley floor diagonally, moving southwest to northeast;

fourteen days to cover 62.5 miles. That averages out to a little better than 4.4 miles a day. While at first appearance that may seem easy enough, in addition to the uncompromising heat, the exceptional geographic variations are exacting, inflicting unusual hardship upon the body.

Buck and I entered Death Valley at an altitude of 1,286 feet, heading for Nemo Crest at 5,318 feet. That would be a serious 4,032-foot ascent, more than three times the height of the Empire State Building, within a 15-mile stretch. A 24-mile continuous descent would then take us down to Stove Pipe Wells Village and the campground where we placed the camper. Then we'd follow a relatively flat terrain for another eight miles, going 89 feet below sea level, our lowest point of the walk, before climbing again a 14.5-mile stretch up to Daylight Pass, at 4,317 feet. That would be an overall climb of 8,438 feet, all done in two weeks!

The first 16 miles in Death Valley did not bring an immediate change in the landscape. The ribbonlike road continued toward the Panamint Range, and it did seem strange that at the same time I was walking the searing asphalt I could see snow-covered Telescope Peak standing in the distance against a cloudless blue sky.

But the long ascent toward Nemo Crest was simply more of the same Sierra Nevada view that I had been surrounded with at Walker Pass two weeks before. The vegetation was sparse, and what survived was as dry as the stems used in dried-flower arrangements. An occasional yucca plant with long spiky leaves towered over me, but for the most part the landscape was barren and strewn with crumbling rocks. Even the lizards dared not venture out from under them.

But one rare day Bucky spotted a scarce Panamint daisy, highly valued in the park. I found him turning around a bush of bright, yellow flowers that was almost his height. He may have sensed an underground water pocket, responsible for the growth of the plant, and was looking for a way to get to it.

In addition to the temperature, which caused me to perspire

*Looking forward to the trip,
but with some apprehension*

All photos by Alex Hanuse

*Bucky
at Kern River*

*Sand dunes
at Death Valley*

Snowstorm at
Goldfield Summit,
Nevada

In the gondola.
I have gotten rid of
my fear of height.

A Ute Indian, Utah

Ruth and Bucky, Elk Springs, Colorado

Crossing paths with the Olympic runner, Hayden, Colorado

Buck and Farla, Nashville, Tennessee

Buck, in 24 degrees below zero weather in Knoxville, Tennessee

Old railroad bed, Virginia

*At a private zoo,
Natural Bridge, Virginia*

*I was invited
to participate in
the Flag Day ceremonies,
Baltimore, Maryland.*

Invitation to a ride,
Philadelphia, Pennsylvania

cor.tinually, the extreme changes in elevation presented a tremendous physical challenge, and my knees weren't up to it.

I'd had little warning that my knees were vulnerable, at least none to which I'd paid attention. I'd had a chronic needle-sharp pain along the sciatic nerve, running from the center of the right hip down the leg into the heel, but I'd got used to it and for the most part ignored it. More recently I'd developed a tiring ache between the shoulders at the top of the spine. The continual pain from both conditions drained my energies. Way back in Santa Cruz I'd decided to try to get relief with a massage. I'd stepped off the road and entered a phone booth to look for a masseuse in the yellow pages. There I read, "Close Encounters, for ladies and gentlemen the ultimate relaxation," and "Rosalie's Magic Fingers, house calls 24 hours," and decided that neither was exactly what I was looking for.

But here in the valley I'd noticed something new, a distracting though not yet painful discomfort in both knees, especially the right one. When that knee was called upon to carry my weight, I felt a new and strange sensation, like carbonated bubbles, in the center of the right knee socket. It didn't hurt but at the same time it certainly wasn't pleasant. I tried to avoid pressuring the knee but that turned out to be impossible, so I proceeded slowly.

On the second day of climbing Nemo Crest, a sharp pain shot abruptly through my right knee. I gave in to it and went down on the road. I got to my feet again and continued, but even more slowly, easing my way up that hill, giving the greatest burden to my left knee. The next day it, too, gave out. What a predicament! I was only 600 miles into a 3,900-mile walk, only two months into an eighteen-month journey.

I put in a call to my physician in San Francisco and described my symptoms. There was a pause, then he questioned, "Have you increased your intake of citrus?" Had I! While walking through the San Joaquin Valley, citrus fruit was already ripening on the trees and I had really indulged in it. The sweet juice of tree-ripened oranges quenched my thirst, and for two weeks I'd eaten almost nothing else.

"Okay," he advised, "you've created an imbalance. Get hold of some calcium tablets and replace what you've lost in your joints."

Good advice, but if you've ever been in Death Valley, you know you can't buy calcium tablets. I started immediately on cottage cheese until I was fed up with it, then I tried chicken bones, gnawing through the soft gristle on the ends and working my way on up the woody sections of the bone. I found a bowl-shaped rock and a smaller round one, and using them as mortar and pestle I ground eggshells into a granular dust and ate them by the gritty spoonful.

These did the job until much later when I could buy calcium tablets. Believe me, all the symptoms I described disappeared.

Meanwhile, Buck and I kept walking the long lonely trail across the dry valley floor, and here more than any other place I used measures of the mind to get me through, ten feet at a time, a hundred feet at a time. Other than the ravens, those large shiny black birds that flew in from the cliffs of the range foraging for food, or an occasional lizard skittering over a rock, the rarity of encounters with other life out here made me realize more than ever how dependent Buck and I were upon one another.

My first encounter with a wild inhabitant of the valley wasn't with a bighorn sheep, as I had hoped, but with a burro. We came upon him standing right in the middle of the road, a black mulelike animal about the size of a small horse. He proceeded to amble toward us, with evident friendliness, coming close enough to rub his nose against my pockets, clearly indicating high interest in their content—Buck's biscuits. And it was surprising that at the same time, a ranger on a routine check in a park vehicle happened by and stopped.

After asking if I needed assistance he inquired. "You're not feeding the burro, are you?"

"No," I replied, "but I have a biscuit I can give him."

"It's not permitted, ma'am."

"Why is that?" I asked with curiosity.

"We're having a problem with them here. We're moving them out of the monument. They really don't belong here, and they endanger the native animals. They eat their food."

"Where are they from?"

"Brought in by prospectors around 1900. A couple of dozen escaped or were turned loose, and they multiplied. Now there are more than two thousand here, and they're a nuisance to the park."

"They look so friendly . . ."

"Well, when that friendly guy starts grazing, he doesn't leave before he's eaten every plant around, roots and all. It's not like the bighorns. They eat, then move along, leaving enough so that the vegetation grows back. But the burros are greedy and consume everything in sight. The bighorns have to retreat farther and farther into the hills to find food. That's why nobody sees them anymore."

"So what can you do?"

"We auction the burros off to farmers, or to families who will give them good homes. They keep them for their kids or as pets, just because they like them. But there are also groups that want the burros here. They buy them, and, who knows, they may even bring them back . . . it's endless."

During our stay in the valley we heard a lot about the burro problem. Some feel they deserve some kind of naturalization after eighty years in the valley. On the other hand, do the bighorns, which are indigenous, deserve to be confined to smaller and smaller areas, like the Indians on reservations?

The extraordinary heat in the valley created a need for a change in logistics. Buck and I usually traveled light, with just a few extra rations in my pocket for both of us, but the problem of our dependence upon drinking water in areas of extreme drought and blistering heat was assigned to Alex. Before this I'd depended upon various sources for water. In or near towns and cities I would stop at a service station or café, and even in undeveloped areas I could count on a country store. Here, in the heat of the desert, where shade is almost nonexistent, Alex planted jugs of water at intervals along the side of the road. He would scout ahead and return to tell me, "Up ahead six miles, you will find at the side of the road a jug of water and a bowl [usually an empty cottage-cheese tub] for Buck."

That worked fine until the day we came to the spot on the road where our water should be, but it was gone, both jug and bowl. After that, in order to avoid the theft of our precious water, Alex would return and say, "Six miles up the road you'll find a boulder. If you look to the right you'll see a ravine and if you enter that ravine you'll see on the left a bush. Behind that bush you'll find a jug and bowl." The water problem became a treasure hunt, and it worked.

In February the valley was unseasonably hot, 98 degrees. I felt the sun directly overhead, and the hair on my head was no protection from the penetrating heat. At a tourist center I bought a cheap straw hat that resembled a Mexican sombrero. The wide brim shaded my shoulders and the high stack ventilated my scalp. It provided great relief. I tried one on Buck but he wouldn't wear it. The only other shade on the road was to be found under the water tanks put there for tourists' boiling radiators. Buck would find them before I did, and when I caught up with him he'd be in the small patch of shade under the tank and I'd crowd in and join him.

At Stove Pipe Wells Village, a tourist center 40 miles into the valley, we had parked the camper only a few yards from the Sand Dunes, a most spectacular natural formation. From the doorway of our Home Sweet Home those dunes, created by winds carrying particles of rock across the valley, were fantastic sculptured mounds of sand. The mesquite trees that grew from the top of some of the dunes seemed like debris brought in by the last storm or high tide, but of course that was impossible in this dry land. From where we were, little evidence of life could be seen, but in the morning Buck and I took a walk between the dunes and discovered evidence of unexpected nocturnal activity. Between low bushes of pickle-weed, with their strings of picklelike stems, and the small inkweed bushes, which smell faintly like fish, multiple tracks of lizards, sidewinder rattlesnakes, and kangaroo rats attested to heavy traffic during the lower night temperatures. Quite understandably those animals can rarely be seen during day, as the ground temperature sometimes reaches 200 degrees. And I can tell you it's true that eggs can be fried on the overheated rocks.

Buck has more scars from our journey, more visible tell-tale souvenirs, than I do, but these may be the result of the greater distance he traveled. While at the end of our trek I had walked 3,900 miles, Buck covered many, many more, always running ahead or behind me, checking out things of interest to him, which seemed to be everything. It appeared that he covered at least ten times more distance than I did in any given day, and that's a conservative guess. Ten times the 3,900-mile journey! "Why," Alex concluded, "that's 39,000 miles, or equal to his walking around the globe one and a half times!" No wonder he carries the scars. And Death Valley was no exception.

One incident that scarred him stands out in my mind, linked as it is with Death Valley. Buck had been chasing prairie dogs all morning. In spite of the sizzling heat he wouldn't give up. And those burrowing rodents played tricks on him. They have a veritable network of underground tunnels through which they easily eluded him. "Chi-chi-chi," one called, standing in its hole. Buck thought it called to him. He plunged across the sand and dived feetfirst at it but that darn prairie dog knew what it was doing. It ducked in the nick of time, leaving Buck salivating into its hole, frustrated and haggard. "Chi-chi-chi," Buck picked up his ears and charged again, skidding to a stop over the dog's hole.

The hole collapsed and Buck went with it. I heard him yelp with pain and leap backward. I looked in horror. There in the sandy soil was a rattler, still coiled from its attack. Buck lowered his head between his paws and clawed his nose trying to scratch the wound away, but the damage was done and the venom took its action. As I watched, he started to stagger, whimpering in pain, and I took his muzzle in my hands; on the side of his nose I saw a swelling the size of a quarter, and enlarging.

"Oh, Buck, what do we do now?" I cried in consternation, and I watched in dread as the poison did its work. Buck tried to stay on his feet, but couldn't. Before my eyes he fell to the ground and I watched his joints jerking as they stiffened. Small bubbles formed on his lips, his eyes glazed over, and as he looked at me distantly I thought he was gone.

There are those times when communication between two individuals are transmitted unaccountably. This was one of those times. Alex inexplicably returned early. He found us on the road, me bent over a lifeless dog, palpating joints that had gone rigid. We wrapped Buck gently in a blanket; he gave no resistance. We offered him some water, but he seemed not to notice it was there, so I took some on my fingers and let it dribble through his teeth; I knew he had to be thirsty. Together we put him on the back seat of the car and went to find a vet. The closest one would be in Trona, we were told. That was 70 miles away. We made it in fifty-eight minutes. To our dismay, however, there was no vet in town and no one knew where we'd find one. In desperation Alex ran into a medical office, but when the office nurse realized that the patient was a dog, she all but threw him out.

During all this, I'd noticed an almost imperceptible change in Buck's eyes. The glazed look was lessening. Almost afraid to hope, we watched carefully. It was true. I took more water

on my fingers, and although Buck's nose was swollen gro-
tesquely, he allowed me to part his teeth just a little to dribble
the water onto his tongue. Alex and I exchanged glances of
silent anticipation. If sheer will would pull him through, we
knew that together we would make it.

Buck lifted his head just a little and dropped it again heavily.
A small sign, but we were pulling for him and he knew it.
That night we took turns sitting with him, feeding him water
on our fingers, letting him know we believed he'd make it,
and he repaid all our efforts by showing he was trying. By
morning his eyes were unmistakably clearer and he could lift
his head. We put a little meat in his mouth but he didn't want
it. Then we noticed that he was trying to lift his shoulders as
though to stand, but he fell back. Still, he'd tried. We held
our breath, afraid to encourage him, not wanting him to
spend his energy.

But Buck's a sturdy dog, not willing to stay down any longer
than necessary. Anxiously we watched him struggle to raise
his shoulders and fall again, but he persisted, struggling
pathetically to get his legs under him. He fell back, panting,
but he was determined and we saw it. So fearfully, worried we
might not be doing the right thing, we cheered him on. He
got his front legs under him at last and tried to stand and he
couldn't, but he was impatient to be well, so he pushed up on
those wobbly legs and we reached out to support him. I
learned later that rattlesnake bites are not necessarily fatal
although most often they are. I believe it was Buck's good
health and his fighting will to survive that eventually pulled
him through. Buck took a few unsteady steps before he lowered
himself shakily to the floor. But he was down by choice and
willing to take a rest. We knew then he'd make it.

Well, Buck and I survived Death Valley, and on February
28 we crested Daylight Pass, at the midsouthern border of
Nevada, having walked 608 miles in California, the most

mileage we were to walk in any one state. By now we thought we'd handled all the contingencies of the road. There couldn't possibly be that much more to take us by surprise. I laugh about that now.

SIX

......•.....•.•.....•.•....•...•...•....•••.....•

In Pioneer
Territory

When Buck and I came to the California-Nevada border, the
first of the state borders that we would cross on our thirteen-
state journey, we were greeted by a sign riddled with bullet
holes, "Welcome to Nevada."

I'd been to Nevada before. Several times I'd come in by
commercial airline, and once I'd skimmed close to the Nevada
countryside in a single-engine plane. Other times I'd driven
through fast, in a hurry to get someplace else. But I never felt
I knew Nevada. I always had the notion, here as well as at the
other state lines, that simply stepping over an imaginary line
would somehow cause things to be different. And it seems that
many Americans feel that way. During our walk, no matter
where we were, people were curious. "How is it over there?"
"Are we really different?" "How do we measure up?" is what
they wanted to know.

Everywhere we went I found a curiosity to know how it is in
another place in the nation, although it was not always strong
enough to send people looking. I met old-timers in Nevada

who had never been to see a mountain right close by. I talked
with families in Virginia, living within twenty miles of Washington, D.C., who never had gone there, and some in New
York who couldn't even imagine the beauty of the dry purple
sagebrush in an isolated western desert. And yet it seemed it
didn't matter how deep one's local roots went, there was always
way down inside an even greater pride that came from being
American.

Before we left, Alex had asked me, "Will we need special
papers to cross the state borders?" I was surprised at first until
I realized; that question arose from his experience living on
another continent. If you drive 600 miles in Europe, which is
about the distance Buck and I had just walked in California,
you might pass through four nations, some of them smaller
than most of our states. Travel between countries there is also
complicated by different languages and currency and a need
for border papers.

Here, by contrast, Buck and I simply stepped over an
undetectable line and I didn't even have to learn Nevadan.

Nevada was put on the map when the Comstock Lode with
its vast deposits of precious metals was discovered. This
brought fortune seekers from all over the land. But then the
gold and silver ran out, and people left as quickly as they'd
come. As a result, Nevada today is one of the least populated
of our fifty states, with an average of only seven persons per
square mile. Most of that population is crowded in and around
the glitzy gambling towns of Reno and Las Vegas. To attract
people back to Nevada, the state created two industries. In
1931 divorce and gambling were made legal. As a result,
tourism is now one of the major sources of revenue. And in
Nevada everything goes. Gambling, prostitution, split-second
marriage and divorce, all are legal. And it seems as though
the gambling spirit is so persuasive that Nevadans will gamble
on anything. They even bet on me! They took odds we
wouldn't make it! Well, if Buck and I had known it at the time
we would have placed our money on a winning thing. We

knew we'd make it. As a matter of fact, as rough as it got, I never once really doubted that we would make it to the end.

But the rest of Nevada is made up of stretches of starkly uninhabited desert land where only the wildlife can survive the bleak aridity. And yet over the next 93 miles in which we wound our way from Beatty, near the center of the southern border, up through the middle of the state, in and out of the old gold-and-silver-mining towns as far as Goldfield and Tonopah, we were welcomed by an unexpected rousing celebration of people. Across those miles in the barren regions of the Sagebrush State, in speeches, parties, and dinners, it seems we met them all. We were light-years from Reno and Las Vegas, those neon-flashing entertainment centers, hundreds of empty miles from their dazzling hotels done up in mirrored, Greek-statued, multifountained décor. Yet here, in the middle of the desert, so far from those places that plays host to the glamorous and famous in star-studded, lavishly feathered, bare extravaganza—a solitary lady walked in out of the desert with a dog, and they were treated as though they were celebrities. By the time we'd walked that stretch of the road and out again, if there was anybody left in the desert that we hadn't met or anybody who hadn't heard of us, well they must have been living in a cave.

On March 23 Buck and I headed for the town of Beatty, Nevada, only 12 miles north of Death Valley. It's a dusty place, with an aura of the lawless Old West still lingering about it. A few old-timers still live there, but most of the resident families in Beatty are there, on the west side of town, because of the employment at the military installations to the east, out in the desert. I saw a few weathered in-need-of-paint houses and many mobile homes, temporary houses for temporary people. Beatty is a gambling town, really an adult town, as there is very little for young people to do—no movie houses, no bowling lanes, no swimming pool, not even a lake.

But gaming is everywhere. In Nevada it's darn near impossible to pass by a gas station, a convenience store, or the like without hearing the clamor of the bell-ringing, light-flashing one-armed bandits waiting inside every public door. And there's no shortage of hopefuls waiting to feed those gluttonous machines. Buses roll perpetually over the border from California on their way to the Reno and Vegas gambling capitals. Beatty is the first chance to gamble once one crosses the Nevada state line. The buses idle while normally conservative coupon-clipping travelers rush into dingy cafés, elbow their way to the noisy machines, and, taking monopoly on several at a time, pump money into the slots and yank away at the chrome-plated handles, knowing all the while that the machines will win in the end.

On my way through town I stopped in the shade of an old wooden porch to talk to a gray-haired woman standing in the doorway of her small cluttered shop. It was filled with articles for tourists, items like ceramic salt and pepper shakers, some at the very edge of pornography. There was little animation left in her weary, wrinkled frame. While shrugging over her shoulder at the two youngsters playing behind the counter, she told me that she was raising "those two." They were her grandchildren, abandoned to her by their mother. Her daughter had run off "with who knows who, or to what"—perhaps to high-wage employment, waitressing in a Vegas casino. And it was she who told me that a big attraction for youngsters in town came from "foolin'" with drugs, although as my walk went on, I would discover that this practice was not exclusive to Beatty.

To get away from this depressing dialogue, I stepped back into the sunlight, got my bearings, and then headed out of town, down a dusty street where the curbs crumbled.

By striking contrast the highway leading north into the desert was impeccable. It was paved with a red rock material that looked as though it had been taken from the surrounding hillside, ground into pea-sized pebbles, and then laid down in a narrow two-lane strip that ran over the godforsaken land. And it blended in so well with the landscape that I wondered if that choice of material was intentional, as it certainly would make the road less visible from the air. According to my maps, I was surrounded by secret, off-limits military ranges: the Atomic Energy Nuclear Testing Site, Nellis Air Force Range, and the Tonopah Test Range. I had been told by one congressman that the military is now the number two source of revenue in Nevada, putting it second only to gambling, with which it seems to have much in common.

I felt extremely vulnerable walking Highway 95. For 79 miles we'd have to follow the western border of those military zones that are so effectively concealed that even though I strained my eyes I could see nothing, not even a clue to the vast military power and weaponry that I know exist out there. I wondered what secret nuclear testing had taken place recently. What radioactive dust could be blowing in the wind at that very moment. If it were not for my well-worn maps and the frequency of the fighters and bombers screaming across the sky, splitting the air with rolling sounds like thunder, leaving thin trails in an otherwise cloudless sky, I wouldn't even have suspected the presence of such installations. That noise always brought Buck running to my side. Looking back, I can't help but wonder what advanced technical instruments of war were out there in that lifeless region. Weapons that are only now whispered about, like the radar-evasive super-secret Stealth F-19, with its radar-absorbing skin, which operates over these stellar western skies only at night, when they are hidden from Soviet spy satellites. The weapons are there to protect us, I was told. In that system of destruction is our protection against being overrun. And yet those undercover safeguards undisputedly go on gambling with your very life and mine.

Then Buck and I entered into internal regions of Nevada where the seemingly endless desert blends together in tones of little variation. The muted tans, grays, and blues meld from one tint to another with little delineation; the omnipresent sage trembles in the wind, and the yuccas stand like sentries against a horizon of easily rolling hills. In that lonesome land there is a harmony so peaceful, so utterly tranquil, that at times I could feel that my environment and I were one.

We were only ten miles north of Beatty when I noticed that Buck was having problems with his feet. The highway sloped steeply and was grooved on the edge in tight ridges. These ridges, undoubtedly, I thought, were intended to allow rapid runoff from occasional flashfloods. But the ridges and the hot rough surface played havoc with Buck's paws. He really had no choice, though. He had to walk the roadbed or step off into the hot alkaline soil. It wasn't long before the pads on his feet split open and he began limping. That evening while Buck was sleeping in one of his favorite positions, lying on the ridge of his spine, he had all four feet stretched straight above him, and I had a good opportunity to notice what looked like a crack in one of his paws. I took a closer look and found, not one crack, but a number of angry-looking splits that penetrated down into the pads on all four of his feet. Miles of walking rough roads and blistering desert soil had made for some mighty painful paws. Deep in the cracks a bloody liquid oozed to the surface. Still Buck was determined to continue the journey. The next day he fought to join me on the road and never once complained. As it happened, that day I spoke with students at Beatty's schools, and when they asked, as people always did, about how Buck was doing, I told them about the trouble he was having with the pads on his paws. Later, when I stopped in at the office to leave my mailing address for students who wanted to write, the school secretary, who had heard about Buck's problem, asked, "Have you tried bag balm on his feet?"

I'm a city girl and hadn't the foggiest notion what bag balm was, so she explained.

"We use it on the cows. We rub it on our palms before

milking them, keeps their udders soft. Prevents cracking."

If it would help Buck, I was for it. "Where can I buy it?"

"Don't worry, we have plenty in the house."

She picked up the phone and sure enough, her husband left what he was doing and came right over to the school with a gob of yellow salve neatly wrapped in a square of aluminum foil. "Take some in your hand like this," he instructed, "and rub it into his paws. Should do the trick."

That night Buck got the treatment. I massaged bag balm into his paws, into the pads and down between his toes, though I was not completely convinced that a sticky salve could heal cracks that penetrated so deeply. But I put it on and Buck started to lick it off.

"Leave it on, Buck," I scolded him. And he did. Buck knows when he needs help, and over the miles, we came to have an unspoken trust and confidence in one another. We each instinctively knew that if the chips were down, the other would be there.

Amazingly the very next day his feet were better. That was miracle stuff. So for weeks every night I rubbed bag balm into his paws until they were completely healed. It almost took the surface off my fingers because by this time Buck's paws were so rough it was like rubbing sandpaper of the coarsest grade. His nails were now worn down short and the hair that normally grows between his toes was rubbed away. The pads were thicker, raising his nails higher off the ground and so the nails grew longer that way, a simple adaptation of his body to the conditions to which he was exposed.

We were able to continue from Beatty to Goldfield, where we were heading, which is a distance of about 70 miles. Buck and I were well on our way when we came upon an isolated house surrounded by desert and nothing else. A driveway led up to an attention-grabbing pink ranch-style house, the kind you'd find in any suburban neighborhood. But this house stood alone. It was set way back off the road on the slant of a low hill, and identifying letters that could easily be seen from the sky were emblazoned behind it on the hill. "Salley's Ranch" was surrounded by a huge parking lot that made me wonder what kind of traffic Salley could possibly expect out there in the middle of that hot barren land, with not even a bush between the road and the house to interrupt the monotony of the sandy desert ground. And off on the side of the road, a small weathered carcass of a single-engine plane was resting at a tilt on a damaged wing. That plane wasn't going anywhere and hadn't for a while, but apparently at one time it had attempted a landing on the short, almost undiscernible airstrip to the right. It looked like Salley's Ranch expected a lot of road and plane traffic to stop by.

That evening my curiosity got the best of me so I asked a couple sitting in a café, "What is that, Salley's Ranch, down the road?" and they told me, "Salley's is one of *those* places." I should have known, Nevada is not only the nation's marriage and divorce capital—it takes zero days to get married there, and only six weeks to get divorced—and a gambling state, but it's also the state where prostitution is legal, regulated by the state. This industry does not get as much publicity as the casinos, but titillating pamphlets like "The Brothels of Nevada," found in most tourist shops, provide reviews like those given to restaurants in many travel guides. In those brochures Salley's Ranch and others of its kind are given ratings on the specialties of the house. A preselection can be made according to the names of the hostesses, their particular skills, prices, activities, and even the décor of their rooms, some done up in Victorian, some in modern, and others mirrored wall-to-wall.

Eight miles from Goldfield, Nevada, we were moving right along. When we'd started out that day, warm breezes blew from the south pushing us in the direction we were going, which made walking unusually easy and comfortable. It was warm, so I'd taken off my sweatshirt and tied the sleeves around my waist, keeping on only a lightweight, multicolored cotton jacket, which I liked because it made me highly visible on the road. I didn't notice when the winds first shifted, but after a while I put my sweatshirt back on because I was getting cool. The winds had spun around and were gusting in from the north, and the sky was quickly turning dark and threatening. Now the winds stuck us head-on with increased velocity, gusting, I estimated at about 40 miles per hour.

I lowered my head and leaned into the wind, and before long I noticed tiny particles collecting on the navy stripe on my jacket, maybe pollen, I thought, carried from over the desert. I brushed them away with the back of my hand but they came with greater frequency, and to my amazement I saw that they were crystals—delicate white crystals of snow. I couldn't believe it. The flakes began to accumulate on my chest, my face, and my hair. The snow collected faster and had soon formed a layer on my clothing, and I began to feel the chill of it. Buck caught flakes on his nose, causing him to stop and sneeze, which shook the flakes from his ears. But soon he, too, wore a mantle of white on his shoulders, so that every few feet or so he stopped and shook his body.

We'd been walking on sun-heated rocky terrain and at first the snow had melted, but now it was falling rapidly and I could no longer see the horizon. My view of the landscape was limited to the few feet around me. I could no longer tell where the road was. A smooth white blanket covered the ground, and except for the occasional car that went by, laying down a strip of tire tracks, I couldn't tell if we were walking at the edge of the road or on the road itself. If traffic had been heavier, we could have followed the car tracks, but the falling snow rapidly covered the trail, and I no longer knew if we had perhaps wandered off into a field so far from the road that we couldn't find our way back.

Buck was frantic. He ran around, shaking the snow from his back, lifting one foot then another, trying to get away from the cold. This was a new experience for him and he didn't like it.

The freezing white world we were in so distracted him that I had a devil of a time keeping him off the road, even though I wasn't sure where the road was.

The cold weather turned to freezing. I took my sweatshirt off again and struggled with Buck to get his legs into the sleeves, pulling the hood over his head and zipping it over his chest. "Come on, Buck, we've got to run for it." We ran toward what I hoped was the summit, and the run generated heat in the two of us. My lungs were bursting when I saw the sign "Goldfield Summit," and from what I remembered, Goldfield itself should be about two miles the other side of it. We hustled along, our breath blowing in front of us, and when I saw the first gray outlines of houses in town, I knew that Buck and I had made it.

Rivulets of water streamed through the steam on the café windows. I opened the door and let Buck in without asking permission from anyone and shoved him under a table. The room was heated by a potbellied stove and the snow on our clothes started to melt, dripping onto the wooden floor, creating an ever-expanding puddle. A man in a white cook's apron looked through a window from the kitchen and then came and stood over us with a scowl. "Boy," he snapped, "clean that up," and a lanky youngster rushed over with a mop and pushed it around us while a group of men at a long bar on the other side of the room turned around and stared. Behind the bar stood a collection of bottles and old mugs in front of a mirror, yellow with smoke and age. The men had the rough, unkempt look that I expected old-time mining prospectors to have. I could imagine that those rugged, bearded men had just ridden into town from their claims to compare and wager nuggets of gold. "You going to belly up or just talk about it?" one grumbled to a new arrival. They stood leaning back on the bar and stared at us for a while, taking us in without saying a word. Then one turned back to the bar, poured a shot and downed it, and the others slowly followed suit and resumed a gruff discussion, mostly about the weather.

One of them, however, just kept gawking. He couldn't take his squinty eyes off us. He wore an old black fur cap pulled down low over his ears, which left a small oval of a red and weathered face exposed. He had a thick black and gray grizzled beard that ran down over his chest, and his mouth hung open, revealing gums from which the teeth were mostly missing. A dark overcoat hung down to and covered the tops of his heavily oiled black boots. He looked as if he could have just stomped in from the outer regions of the Yukon. I was ravenous and in need of heat, so I gulped my steaming soup while slipping chunks of two cheeseburgers under the table for Buck. Nobody said anything to us, but that man continued to ogle us. I was amused. I was used to being the observer, but this time I was the object of his speculations. He was trying hard to make sense of the curious sight he was seeing, a lightly dressed lady with a dog wearing a sweatshirt who had come in out of the storm covered with snow! He just couldn't take his eyes away and he was still gaping like that when at last we were dry and warmer and left the café, stepping back outside into the glare of the sun.

It wouldn't take long to walk through Goldfield; I could see that. From where we were standing I could look down the main street through town and out the other side. We would be following the path of a superhighway which, incredible as it seemed, would take us in and out of one small town after another through some of the most deserted regions of the nation. And surprisingly we were only 200 miles almost due east of San Francisco, where we'd started. If we'd run over the top of the mountain and straight on through the deserts as a roadrunner might, we could have been on this same spot two months earlier. But because we had gone those 300 California miles south and then had come back up north again, we had traveled for three months instead of one, and 600 miles instead of 200. As a result, I was now on a third pair of jogging shoes. Buck was still on the very same pads!

I cast a guick glance around Goldfield. Maybe eight hundred people, I estimated. That is, if I didn't miss anybody. From here our itinerary would take us to Tonopah, 25 miles up the road, and after that I'd come to Ely, another 168 miles. In between those communities there's nothing. Absolutely nothing except a few prairie dogs, maybe, and eternally more desert. A few ravens flew in to visit us occasionally. They are the biggest of the black birds, almost two feet long, with feathers so black they shimmer with an iridescent purple. They would come in for a landing not too far away and comically take a few bold steps right along with us. I'd toss a few of Buck's morsels from my pocket to them, which they quickly picked up, and then they would fly back into the hills. Those monogamous birds pair up and marry for life. That gives them a zero divorce rate in a state known for the opposite extreme.

Goldfield, Tonopah, and Ely are the "big" towns we'd travel through, the biggest of them not having more than five-thousand residents. Our route did not take us into Reno and Las Vegas, and even if it had been more direct to go through either one of them, I'd still have preferred the desert. In the remaining 252 miles while walking Nevada, we would come to a few other spots like Blackjack and Blue Jay, but even though I knew for a fact I was standing on the very spot the map told me those places lie, I'll be darned if I could find them.

Most of the United States is uninhabited! I know it is because I walked it. But it sure doesn't seem like it when you grow up in a community of any size at all, or when you hear about all the poeple who go hungry for want of food. In Nevada that lack of food seems darn near impossible. There are endless stretches of wide-open spaces, with maybe a few cattle grazing here and there or an occasional herd of black-tailed antelope leaping over the range. You can't help but wonder why, since there's not a shortage of land on which to grow food, there is such a shortage of doing it. Buck and I had just walked hundreds of miles in California over land that had once looked pretty much like this. California was and still is a desert, but it turned its deserts into farms, and with the help of irrigation the state raises every crop that's known and grown in the nation, with the exception of tobacco. In California we'd walked through apple, pear, and prune orchards, cabbage, onion, tomato, cotton, and rice fields—you name it, it's there. But out here, nothing. Nevada doesn't have water. Its rainfall is not even four inches per year, which makes it the driest state in the nation, but of course we're limiting our discussion to water; the consumption of alcohol, if not *the* highest, must at least be close.

But Buck and I were standing in the mud in Goldfield at the end of March, and the facts that San Francisco and Goldfield are very close in latitude and that each was born from a gold rush are about all they seem to have in common.

Goldfield exploded onto the map when gold was discovered in its hills. But when the gold ran out, so did the people, almost as fast as they'd come, leaving behind them an enormous hotel and a shell of a town, so that today Goldfield is almost a ghost town. But not quite. There are people here who want to make certain that Goldfield doesn't die, those who want to hold on to this remembrance of the past, who love it for what it is and what it represents.

The main street was deserted when we arrived. As we set off down it, I imagined how it might have been when the gold seekers rushed into town. We passed a few old Victorian houses and storefronts boarded up and locked. Once the stores' dusty shelves were stocked with miner's needs, the shovels, picks, and pans for screening and sifting the soil. I could almost see those rugged, bearded men throwing cotton sacks of buckwheat, tins of coffee and beans into leather pouches strapped onto the sides of a mule and could almost hear the

clippity-clop of hooves as they headed down this road and
back up into the hills.

A few more blocks down the street and Buck and I came to
the red-brick four-storied Goldfield Hotel. We climbed the
stairs and looked through a window. Years ago, money had
not been spared to create a magnificent style. But it made me
feel lonely to look in on the enormous marbled lobby now
vacant except for the dust-covered piano standing alone. Not
even echoes remained of the music or of the rowdy laughter
when men and women exchanged nuggets for chips and
fortunes were gambled away. The dull mahogany paneling
and banisters told me of the former elegance, but the hotel
was old and shabby, and the empty pigeonholed registration
desk did not make one feel welcome. Buck and I sat down
close together on the broad front steps. I put my arm around
him while he cheered me up by nuzzling against my chin,
and I looked over the town.

A thin trail of smoke puffed from a rusty elbow of pipe
jutting from the roofline of one of the old slapped-together
miners' shacks. A few still remain scattered over the hills, as
randomly, it seems, as the tall desert Joshua trees, whose short
spiny leaves still carried a load of melting snow.

The atmosphere was getting me down, so I stood up and
called to Bucky, and together we went looking for Virginia.
We found her at the Glory Hole Antique Shop, just as Bob
and Helene had told us we would.

Bob and Helene Lowes publish the *Gateway Gazette*, a
small weekly they edit in Beatty, print overnight in Las Vegas,
115 miles away, and distribute in Death Valley and central
Nevada on the following day. Bob and Helene had covered
our progress as Buck and I wound our way across Death Valley
and as we trailed on into the middle regions of Nevada. But
for real speed, a grapevine of information exists out there that
transmits news faster than satellite, it seems. Virginia, the
owner of the Glory Hole, was already waiting for us and it
wasn't long before everybody in town knew that we had arrived.

This was the town's real communication center, and once information reached here, it was broadcast from one person to another. It's not every day, I guess, that a cross-country walker comes strolling into Goldfield, and news of our arrival generated some excitement.

But most of the excitement in town was due to a bigger event. A busload of legislators, reporters, and special guests, including the governor's wife, Bonnie Brian, was expected to pull into town while on a tour to promote Nevada's "Pioneer Country." This region understandably has some difficulty competing with Reno and Las Vegas for tourists.

Well, they invited us to attend their banquet and reception in Tonopah that evening, and suddenly I felt an overdue need for a haircut, and fast. Buck and I had been on the road for three months now. We'd gone through rain and snow and blistering heat and storms of every kind, and my hair looked every bit of it. My immediate question was how do I find a hairstylist in a strange town out in the middle of nowhere? I was used to having Art, a friend in San Francisco, cut and shape and permanent on schedule to keep me looking business-right.

I looked at Buck. In my opinion he had it made. All he needed was a new surveyor's-tape ribbon tied to his collar, and he was ready for the big event. With the exception of the barbed-wire scars, the fade spots on his rump, and a recent tear on his left ear, Buck still looked pretty much the same. His hair wasn't any longer and he wouldn't have cared if it were. Every morning when he awoke, Buck stretched and yawned, shook himself, rattling the chain around his neck, and with his grooming done, he was ready for the road.

For at least thirty-five years, though, I'd followed an early morning routine that included a shower, a careful application of makeup, and a studied arrangement of my hair. Those habits were so firmly fixed I never even gave them a thought. Then I'd slip into a dress or suit and step behind my desk. Now that I was almost 700 miles into a cross-nation walk, I can't believe it but I was still going through that procedure. Except for the dress and desk, of course.

Art wasn't around but I still needed a haircut, so I did what seemed the practical thing to do. I kept my eyes open while I walked, until I spotted a woman with a neat head of hair, coming out of a grocery store. I caught up to her. "Excuse me," I said. "I noticed your hair looks nice." Naturally she looked startled, but I went on, "I badly need a haircut. I'm just passing through your town. Could you tell me, please, who you could recommend."

Her hand flew to her head, patting her hair, and she pointed across the street. "Over there. In that center there's someone. Heard she's the best in town."

I entered the salon. "Who's the best in town in here?"

"I don't know," said the gum-chewing lady in blue jeans, boots, and suede vest, "but I'm the only one in here."

She put me in a chair and grabbed the scissors, but I quickly held up my hand. "Wait. First let me tell you what I want done." And I proceeded to describe in detail how Art had styled my hair. She knew, she said, just what to do, nodding all the time. But as the scissors snipped and the hair flew, I began to wonder.

"The best in town" chattered with the cut. She had been until recently a mayor, an honest-to-goodness pistol-packing one at that, somewhere in the desert. She'd come back into town to make a living.

It wasn't long before I knew a sheep shearer could have done as well. What was left of my hair stuck out in funny wisps where it never had before. I put my hands up to my head and pulled at the tufts, trying to make some of them look longer and blend in with the others. It was hopeless. But as luck would have it, it turned to an advantage: I no longer had to think about the wind messing it up.

I felt strangely not like me at all. But then I decided what the heck, this is the way I look, and then I decided to go the rest of the way. So, though I didn't have a chain to rattle, I came close to imitating Buck. From that day on, every morning after, it was a quick brush of my teeth, a run of my fingers through my hair, and I was ready for the road.

The first time I stepped out with my newly nude face and closely shorn head, the lizards ran to hide. But I knew better and didn't take it personally.

After the banquet that evening I was asked to speak. I described the route that had brought us into town and some of the adventures Buck and I had had along the way. I told them that in my opinion the Nevada desert is one of the most fascinating landscapes in America, and I ended up by inviting them all to come out on the road and walk with Bucky and me.

Afterward, among those who came up to talk were two men, Doug Heller and Andy Demetras. Both were ready to accept my invitation. They were willing to have, not themselves, but their wives, come out and join me on the road. Helen and Alexandria were good sports about it, laughing at their husbands' intentions, and they both accepted, making a decision to walk the 25 miles between Goldfield and Tonopah. I was going to do that section of the road in the next two days, but if I was going to have company, I'd better make it three at least, I thought. After all, Buck and I were getting used to this walking life. We were in great shape now. My leg muscles were hard, my lungs held more air. If there had been a need for it, we could have done that stretch in one day. Twenty-five miles, though, divided by three days still meant better than eight miles a day, which is a heck of a lot when muscles aren't accustomed to it.

But what a bonus for me! In addition to the fun of having two lively companions, Alexandria and her husband, Andy, had a glass-enclosed atrium in their hilltop home, in the center of which was a large hot tub. And so for the next three days, after our miles on the road, that's where we headed. While my friends in California were worrying about my safety,

I was living it up, lying around in the soothing comfort of a warm bubbling Jacuzzi. I never had it so good.

On April 15 I wrote an update to a life-long friend:

My dear Alice,

Alex and I thought Nevada could be a long monotonous journey of emptiness. Not true! After crossing Death Valley, we entered Nevada. We put the camper north of Beatty, and Bucky and I began our walk to Goldfield and Tonopah on Highway 95. The editor of the Beatty newspaper, the *Gateway Gazette*, called ahead of us that we were heading that way and as a result, ever since Goldfield we have been busy. . . .

. . . We were immediately invited to a reception . . . and from that I was asked to address the Rotary Club (yesterday) and the Lions Club (tonight) in Tonopah. Buck and I were interviewed by the local newspapers and the radio, and tomorrow we will be on the local TV. I spoke with youngsters in an assembly, which as you know I love, at the Goldfield school on Tuesday, and will be in the elementary and high schools in Tonopah tomorrow. I will make a public presentation, sponsored by the Chamber of Commerce, at the Convention Center next Tuesday, I gave a presentation and had lunch with the seniors at a center. And we thought this would be a quiet stretch of the road!

The Nye County district attorney's wife, Alexandria, walked the 25 miles from Goldfield to Tonopah with me, doing it in three days. Her friend Helen joined us for two, and to keep up with Alexandria, Helen plans to make up the additional distance on another day farther on down the road. The 25-mile completion and entry into Tonopah were treated like a triumph. And now a group is even talking of a Nye County delegation flying to New York to walk the last miles to the Statue with us.

Andy and Alexandria Demetras have been wonderful, having a dinner for us . . . Helen and Doug have done the same, and at Helen's insistence we made use of her laundry facilities, catching up on mountains of dirty clothes. It is part of our new walking life to search for launderettes, not the easiest to come by in the desert. Doug, an engineer, has gone to great lengths to repair the broken frames of my eyeglasses, which seem to always fall from my pants pockets, which are too shallow. I have so far lost four pair and now buy them in variety stores when we're lucky enough to find one around. I have thought of many improvements I would make in a collection of practical and attractive walking clothes.

Of course, Bucky is a hit everywhere—everyone likes him, and his nose and ears are petted to his happy heart's content.

We have received an invitation to make a detour to Las Vegas with an opportunity to speak with students at the university there, and the Soroptimists, and to meet again with Bonnie Brian to discuss an educational subject for young people. We are considering it. It would require four days to make up upon our return, but Buck and I have the stuff to do it.

We are now walking Highway 6, going back into the uninhabited regions of the desert again. We are heading east toward Ely and have a long stretch ahead of us. Alex and I are in great shape, and Buck is, too [I had not informed family and friends of the most serious health obstacles we all had overcome]. We are all enjoying. Our health is excellent and even improving. So please, don't worry about us. Our experience is like a beautiful novel we will hate to have end. So, Alice, we will simply have to create a sequel!

Your loving friend

After a week in Tonopah, we simply had to move on. Alex had enjoyed the diversion as much as I. But I'm sure that what he would miss most would be those bridge-playing sessions with his new desert partners, whereas after the fast-paced activity I would feel the isolation of the desert more markedly than ever. On April 10 we left Tonopah, the oasis of lighthearted fun, and headed out into the open desert on Highway 6, for Ely, 168 miles away.

And when Buck and I climbed the last rise in the road, which carried us out of Tonopah over the last hill in town, we looked down into a wide mountain basin over a landscape as austere as the surface of the moon. Our shadows fell in front of us in long slim silhouettes onto a road that cut straight through the middle of the valley and extended all the way across it, rising onto the farthest rim. Buck and I spent day after day walking that road, rising again to the rim of still another basin, where again we looked down on the narrow strip of road leading us somewhere into forever. Those roads drew us on and on over one horizon after another, and it was solitary, and it was beautiful.

Directly ahead of us now was the longest, most isolated total of 324 cactus/sagebrush miles we'd ever encounter again. To the Nevada-Utah state line, we had 237 miles remaining. And after we'd finally make it to the Utah border, we'd still have another 87 desert miles before we'd come to Delta, our first town in Utah as big as perhaps two thousand inhabitants. And believe it, coming in after those weeks in the desert, Delta would look big.

Buck and I headed out to cover the first 49 miles to where my map told me I'd find the community of Warm Springs. We found a small, rusty, steam-spouting creek, bubbling to the surface and seeping back into the sand, and a few dilapidated old wooden buildings. It was all that remained of what had once been a local mineral bath. And we found the landmark I'd now come to expect in these remote regions, the local café. That was it. That's all there was to tell me that I was standing in Warm Springs and that somewhere out in the range where you cannot see at all, people exist and make a living, mostly by raising cattle.

Those local cafés serve the traveler hurrying through. Buck and I could get something liquid, but even more important we could get out of the sun for a while. The cafés also serve the backcountry communities. Families drop by from way out yonder, the kids playing around the pool while the adults pull up to the bar and swap local news. These cafés are part of the grapevine. That's the way for people to keep tabs on what's going on and what's happening to whom. And while it may not be the fastest means of communication, it works. I saw a folded note with Andy's name scribbled on it, pinned against a billboard. It contained a message for him to pick up the next time he happened by.

I had promised to speak at the school, so we detoured into the backland territory to find the Warm Springs School, seven youngsters and their teacher. Later, 67 miles beyond Warm Springs, we came to Currant, another spot on the road with, you bet, a café, where, improbably, a fat brown and white long-horned plaster cow, three times my height, watched over the road. Again we detoured into the back desert, this time 19 miles, looking for Duckwater and another one-room school, and discovered that even in those most secluded locations, aspirations exist as in any other place. There, in the most insulated area, leading the lessons was Nevada's Teacher of the Year, and I discovered that one of her pupils planned to become an astronaut.

Helen kept her promise to join me again and came out and walked those last 12 miles into Warm Springs with us. She was wrapped up like a mummy in a heavy quilted jacket, a woolen scarf around her neck, and a cap pulled down over her ears. We could easily have passed for sisters. Helen and I picked up where we had left off, talking about many things, even comparing the origin of our names, as both "Helen" and "Elena" have the same root. That simple observation led to the discovery of a coincidence, that one of Helen's daughters was named Elena and, more surprisingly, was married to a young man named Guy. "That's my son's name," I told her. "Don't tell me, Helen, that you also have a Gary in your family."

"We do! Another daughter's husband's name is Gary. But,"

she continued, "I'll bet we have one name in the family you don't have. It's too unusual."

"What is it?"

"Guy's last name is Forrest."

This was really too much. "Helen, that's my son Gary's middle name!"

Between talking up a storm, we also discovered that we both love to sing, and then the miles really flew as Helen and I harmonized in the desert to songs like "Home on the Range."

It was impossible to be with Helen without laughing, which hurried along a need for the convenience-station-of-the-road. We were in an area as flat as a pancake, and the highest of the sage bushes barely came up to my waist. But Helen was undaunted by such matters. (As a matter of fact, compared with the many people who came out and walked with Buck and me, I was the least experienced of all. I learned all that "in the woods" stuff as we went along.)

We wound our way through the brush back away from the road, and Helen kept walking much farther than I. When she returned, I could see that she was carrying something she hadn't been carrying before. As she got nearer, I was astonished to see that she had a suitcase. In the most uninhabited, desolate area—I mean there's *nothing* out there—Helen had found a suitcase. In 324 miles of nothing, where hardly a car goes by, what could be the probability of someone else having been on this exact same spot? And the suitcase hadn't been there for long, as it showed very little signs of weather.

We turned and scanned the desert in every direction, even though there was no place where anyone could possibly be, unless—and we both came to this conclusion with an ominous start—the person was not standing up; and why would anybody be lying down in this godforsaken place, unless—a shiver of fear ran down my spine—the person was injured or dead.

If we had found the suitcase along the side of the road, we might have concluded that someone had stopped to take a break from the monotony of straight-line desert driving and then—although this was stretching matters—might have driven off, accidentally leaving the suitcase behind. But it had been hundreds of yards from the road, and it wasn't logical to think that someone had walked that far into the desert with a suitcase.

"Do you think we should open it?" Helen indicated a respect for someone's privacy.

"Sure, it might be empty. And if not, it could have identification."

Helen pressed her thumb against the latch and it sprang open. Then she lifted the lid, cautiously, fearful of what we might find. Inside were a pair of blue jeans, a very dainty blouse, a few cosmetics, a pink lipstick, some blue eye shadow, a bra and panties, and a wallet with a few coins, but no identification. The suitcase held just the kinds of things a teenage girl might take for a short visit away from home. It was possible that the girl was lying in the brush somewhere, and if so it was totally inconceivable that either Helen or I could leave without being sure. So we went back. And though we circled round and round through the sage, we found no other traces.

When Helen and I returned to Tonopah that evening, we went to the police station and turned the suitcase in. "It happens all the time," the policeman said in a way that implied he wouldn't get used to it, either. "Youngsters come out from everywhere, hitchhiking to get away. And then, well, some . . . just disappear . . ."

It bothered me, but there was nothing else to do. Although I have met a few who claim not to know or to respond to feelings of concern for a stranger, I don't believe it. The skin doesn't grow that thick, although I do suspect it's possible to forget that we have, and will always have, those natural compassions for others. And there is always the chance that by reaching out to those who claim indifference, we can reawaken their natural empathies. For me, I know that it has got to be the most horrible experience in life when one's child disappears.

The next day Helen's last words to me were "Be careful." They had been said by hundreds of others many times before. But always, when I asked, "Of what?" the answers were generally vague: "You know," or "There's a lot happening out there," and left at that, with the implication that whatever it was, it wasn't good. But I walked the roads observantly and I wasn't frightened, not of things, and most certainly not of people. But one day 125 miles northeast of Tonopah, I sensed an unfamiliar danger.

It wasn't unusual for someone to stop. Motorists, assuming that my car had broken down, did it all the time. Even with big Buck they'd offer me a lift and without exception they were kind, well-meaning individuals and families, ready to give me a hand. But something was different this time.

It was the only car we'd seen all morning. He had torn up the road, passing us not fifteen seconds before, and he braked his dark conservative sedan to a rumbling stop on the dusty corrugated road. I saw him adjust the rearview mirror and study the reflection a few moments before he made up his mind and swung the car around and pulled to a rolling stop across from where we sat.

"I'm going your way," he said without asking where we were headed. Instinctively I mistrusted him. The curl of his lip, intended to convey friendliness, didn't match his eyes. His arm hung too casually from the window and his well-groomed appearance looked too calculated. I intuitively felt on guard. Buck felt it and sat up, and I laid my hand on his shoulder— a silent communication, but I knew he understood that we both should be on guard.

"Why don't you get in, young lady, I'll give you a ride." His smooth voice was low-toned and soothing, but I felt a deceit behind the words. I'd be better off taking my chances heading across the open desert than to get into his car.

And then it hit me, the instant connection with a girl and

her suitcase. Had she been running to get away? Is that how
her suitcase came to be dropped so far away from the road?

I felt the skin on my neck crawl and I looked down at Buck,
a large patch of hair on his back standing on end.

"C'mon, girl," he coaxed in a silken drawl. "It's not safe for
you to be out here." He leaned across the seat, and the
passenger's door swung open.

"I'm all right."

"You can get in, it's okay. I wouldn't tell you that if it
wasn't, now would I? Trust me."

It was the last thing I would do. "Thanks, I'm not interested."

His door swung open and one foot stepped out onto the
road. I stood up abruptly and so did Buck. I put my hand on
his collar to appear as though to restrain him, and it worked.
The man stopped. The curve of his mouth turned down and
his voice was mean and angry. "Don't say I didn't warn you,"
he shouted as he slammed the door, made another U-turn,
and sped off down the road.

It was not usual for me to react the way I did. Normally I
meet people expecting to like them and it usually ends up that
way. I can quite quickly make a distinction between something
I may not like that is being done and the person doing it. But
this man had tried a foxy guile to charm me. How many have
accepted his rides and what happened to those who did, I
wondered, shaking off the experience, and then I forgot him.

One week later, on a Sunday, I came to the tan cinder-
block desert church I was looking for. More and more frequently people asked me to stop and talk in one school or
another, or in a church, or in other places where people
gather. They normally called ahead to a friend or relative to
make the arrangements and gave us instructions about whom
to contact so that by the time we arrived we were expected.

The children of this Sunday school class were waiting at the
entrance. They were giggling and shyly peeking down the

road. it usually takes them just a few moments to understand they have no need to feel timid or reserved with me.

Those youngsters had the idea, like many others, that a walk such as Buck and I were taking was too much for most people. That's really not so, I told them. Like anything else, the hardest part was taking the very first step. And after that, it was just a matter of taking one more step at a time.

"Don't you get hot out there?"

"Sure I do, and sometimes cold. But after a while, weather becomes just weather. It's when you're inside looking out that you're more likely to make more of it than it's worth."

Their leader, was enthusiastic. "I want you to meet our pastor," he said, leading me into the church's social room. "There he is. Come with me." He pulled me through small groups of the congregation toward the pastor. But when the pastor turned around, I was appalled. I had not expected to meet the man who a week before had offered me a ride!

Much of the newness of learning to walk the road was now pretty much under my belt. I had more time to notice, observe, and think about what was going on around us. Frequently Buck and I would sit down together on the ground at the side of the road and do just that.

It was two days after leaving Helen that we sat down and watched the spiraling funnels of air called dust devils. We watched those spinning clouds with long tails come out of nowhere and churn across the desert. They twist like a small tornado, changing directions abruptly, and carry dust and branches along with them, while rising into the sky. I always wondered when one would cross our path, or if they would pick up velocity and become full-blown tornadoes that way. If so, could they carry us off with them? There was no predicting what path they would take, and though I was fascinated by their movement, their presence made me nervous. There was no place for us to hide. They skirted around the desert and frequently came close enough so that I could feel the rush of the circling wind. They sucked sand into a vacuum, whipping it across my face and blowing it into my eyes. So I had a plan and kept it in reserve. If one came too close for comfort, I'd throw myself to the ground and pull Buck up close beside me. After that, there was nothing left to do except to hope for the best.

But at least, there was a natural explanation for their presence. A man at the Warm Springs café had told me that heated air from the desert rises, and when it does, cooler air is drawn in from the sides to replace it, carrying dust and debris in with it, creating a whirling mass that spins in circles, moving wildly across the ground and sometimes rising to great heights.

But what happened on another day, nobody has been able to explain. We were between Warm Springs and Currant when I heard an unusual whispering, rustling sound that seemed to come from nowhere. I looked around for the source of it, so close to us, but there was nothing but the dry desert as we had known it for days upon days. Nothing different at all. It could have been the same desert we'd walked five days before, or five more before that. Yet that strange whispering sound persisted around me. Maybe, I thought, it was a small covey of birds hidden among the leaves of the sage. Or maybe it was a hive of bees looking for pollen in the blossoms. Or maybe an army of locusts or crickets hidden from our view. I didn't know and I couldn't see anything; everything was still. And though I knew there were snakes out there, what I was hearing wasn't either the sound of a rattler or that of a buzzard circling overhead.

Then I noticed the small leaves on a bush quiver nervously, just tremble and then stop, and there was silence. Then the leaves of another bush trembled with the same rustling sound, and then another. Those bushes were not in a straight path. They were not even close to one another, and there was nothing, not even a breeze, between them. Again another bush started to tremble with the same twittery sound and abruptly stopped. And then another one. Buck and I stood very still, and the way he cocked his head to the side and lifted his ears, I knew he heard it, too. Whatever it was, it was near enough for me to see that there was absolutely nothing that moved from bush to bush, and yet it passed in front of us. A path of quaking bushes continued across the road, the trembling agitation visible on the bushes on the other side, just twitching, trembling, and rustling, and it went across the desert like that, off into the distance. I don't disquiet easily but I admit that something about that sound made me feel uncomfortable.

Later, as I asked about what I'd seen and heard, no one could give me an explanation. I found none who had ever witnessed anything like it. I cannot believe I have been the only one to have had that experience. I know that it's much more likely that it simply goes unnoticed by those who live there. It's much more likely that my unfamiliarity with the region made me more attentive to the sounds of the bushes and their agitation than those who had been surrounded by desert all their lives.

I spent time trying to recall some clues from things I'd read and heard, anything that would help to give logic to my observation. It was so mysterious that I even surprised myself by playing around a bit with explanations about supernatural powers. I began to understand more fully how more primitive humans had looked to the supernatural to explain what they didn't understand.

I still don't know what happened that day in the desert, and maybe I never will. But I did not dream it. If an explanation comes along, I welcome it.

We were 18 miles from Ely, Nevada. I was looking forward to being in a town again and having the luxury of conveniences like a laundromat and a place to buy milk. Buck was running low on dog food. He had gone through seven twenty-five-pound bags of chow—all that running around whipped up his appetite—but there wasn't an ounce of fat on him.

I saw the badger moving through the brush before Buck did, and it interrupted my thoughts. Buck couldn't see it but he smelled it and stood, one paw raised, at attention. I watched the badger maneuver in the sage. He had sensed Buck and was preparing his escape. Buck jumped into the bushes, sniffing like a hound. The badger moved faster, taking advantage of his superior knowledge of the environment. They couldn't see each other but I could see both, and I could tell that the badger was determined to get away while Bucky was equally determined to get him. But suddenly the badger stood, frozen, and faced in Buck's direction, and I realized that Buck was in danger. If he found the badger, it would put up the fight of its life, now that it had decided to face the intruder, and Buck might not survive. Badgers are mean, powerful killers when they fight and Buck was only ten feet from him. But Buck failed to see him. The badger, having escaped detection, turned and fled. My strategy was to continue walking faster, knowing that since Buck had got lost in California, he would not leave me alone on the road for long, and sure enough, he soon came leaping after me. That fight might have cost him his life.

It was mid-April, and Buck and I were still following Highway 6 in Nevada, cutting through the southern tip of the western section of the Humboldt National Forest. I was accustomed to California's heavy timberlands where the conifers are so thick and tall the sun has trouble getting through. This forest looked nothing like that. There were trees in Humboldt, all right, miles and acres of them, but pines so stunted by drought that the only things they could possibly shade would be smaller than a sparrow.

We were now far from any emergency medical facilities, farther than we would ever be again. So, without saying anything about it, I was frequently observing Alex, looking for any indications that might suggest a need for medical attention before an emergency occurred. But Alex looked well. He wasn't pale or tired. Indeed, he looked healthier now than before we'd left.

In fact, we all did. Buck ran around wearing the alert expression of a dog that feels happy about his life, and he had boundless energy for running over the hills or through the sage or wherever his nose took him exploring. Ever since the incident in California, I had started training him while we walked along the road. Now when I told him "Heel," "Sit," and "Wait," he knew there was a good reason for my saying it, that he would no longer get by with doing as he pleased. I set the limits, and like a child, the respect he developed for me that way sharpened our relationship. Buck was a better dog. And he was just as friendly as ever. He'd now met thousands of people along the way, all of whom had treated him well.

As for me, I was hitting my stride. My face and arms were so deeply tanned I thought I would never lose it. My feet were through with blistering and had never developed a callus. On many days I felt I could walk forever and that I really had it made.

Buck and I came on down out of the Humboldt Forest on April 16, on a cold and blustery day, and walked into a town as depressed as any we would come to again. I had left on this journey across America when the country was still caught up in a deep economic recession, and I could feel the heavy weight of its influence in Ely as we walked through the town.

Until recently, Ely had depended for employment upon its copper mine—one of the largest open-pit mines in the world. But the mine could not compete with cheaper copper production costs elsewhere in the world, so it closed, and of the five thousand town residents, fourteen hundred were out of work.

The wind swept a few leaves along the gutter, but other than that the streets were bare, and every other house seemed to have a For Sale sign tacked onto the fence. I picked up a brochure on our way through town and was startled to see that respectable two-bedroom homes were on the market for as little as $13,000—and not selling! The one hotel was practically empty and the one-armed bandits in the lobby silent.

I had looked forward to Ely as a milestone, our very last town in Nevada. But it was disheartening to notice the cheerless spirit as families faced the bleak outlook of selling off their homes. So Buck and I headed east, out again into the open desert. Now we had only 69 miles left to the Utah state border.

On the first day of spring, and our last day in Nevada, Buck and I were walking a high mountain basin more confidently and more at home with the world than ever before. Way off in the distance, up on the ridge of a hill, we noticed a small cloud of dust and we stood still to watch it. Whatever it was descended into the valley and moved across the basin. Gradually we made out the form of our visitor. A mustang, a spirited wild horse, capered across the valley floor and came to a whinnying halt in front of us. Buck and I watched and barely moved while the mustang pawed the ground with his hoof. Then, tossing his head, he stretched his neck as he shuffled forward and brought his nose up close to Buck's while they sniffed each other, saying who knows what. Very slowly I raised my hand and placed it against his neck. His roan-colored hair was stiff and coarse and very much like Buck's. Then, as quickly as he'd come, he tossed his head, shaking his mane, and with a flip of his tail he pranced off across the desert floor. We watched the dust settle as he left the basin and disappeared into the hills.

Out in the empty vast Nevada desert land there are few distractions to keep you from yourself. I knew when I started my journey that the experience either would strengthen me or do me in. But I had come to grips with it and I learned in the most personal way to give up many of the last remnants of fear. I'd entered Nevada carrying all my concerns into those lonely valleys, and I emerged on the other side having left many behind.

Tomorrow we'd enter Utah.

SEVEN

·······•••·····•••·····•••······•••·····•••······

Mormon Country

Buck and I entered Utah and Mountain Standard time in the last week of April. We'd been blown along for days by cold blustery winds, so I kept my jacket collar pulled up around the back of my neck, where I seemed to feel the cold most. Buds were already forming on the desert sage but showed no sign of opening yet. But a fresh, stirring scent blew in from over the Sevier Desert, and Buck cavorted around me like a new spring lamb.

We were in the highest spirits. For me it was in large measure because we had successfully passed through one of the most isolated regions of our journey. I also could relax somewhat now because Alex had survived it. And while we had crossed the Nevada-Utah line, Buck and I still had more than 90 desert miles to walk before we'd come to Delta, our very first town in Utah. Nevertheless, the end of the desert was now in sight.

I normally walked at a rate of about 3.5 miles per hour. One day a youngster asked me, "Why don't you run instead?"

"Because it would take me longer to cross the country that way." Then, in response to the look of perplexity upon his freckled face, I added, "I can easily walk 15 miles and more in a day, but I haven't trained to *run* that. Besides, by walking, I can enjoy more of what's around me than if I were running."

By walking without rushing, I noticed even the smallest weeds growing in a crack and I sometimes took time to jot down some notes on things I wanted to remember or to sketch a desert flower. By walking, I was able to recognize the road well enough so that the only two times Alex inadvertently put us at the wrong place, I stopped him, thus avoiding a distance we had already walked. And because Alex kept our itinerary, I teased him, "Aren't 3,900 miles enough, without you adding more?"

I had by now a favorite walking stick, a twenty-inch length of wood so smooth and worn by nature that it brought me pleasure just to carry it. Mostly I used it for poking around, to lift the leaves from the head of a mushroom pushing through the ground or to shove aside a branch to get a better view of a paper wasp's nest. I'd once read that for every hour spent in the exercise of walking, one could expect to have extended one's life by an equal amount of time. I already knew I had increased the muscle tone in my back and legs. I was walking taller and straighter and my breathing was regular and deep. And, another happy surprise, my singing voice and range had improved. I could sing "The Happy Wanderer" while walking down the road and hit the highest *Valderi Valderas* without a broken pitch. But I also noticed that my shoulders and arms hadn't kept pace, though if I'd walked on all fours, like Buck, I'm sure they would have. So I devised a number of ways of swinging my walking stick around, rotating it in circles and up behind my back, and in that way I added to my upper-body tone.

Some people might have thought I carried the stick to fend off belligerent dogs, but that wasn't the case. It was my intention to make friends with that kind of dog as well as the friendly ones, and for the most part that's the way it went. The walk taught me that, among other things, America is a land of dogs. About halfway to Provo, I passed an open garage close to the town of Nephi. Inside I could see three orange cats and two large dogs eating from the same bowl. And I thought to myself, that's really nice. Those people have let their animals be at peace with one another. But one of those dogs caught sight of us from the corner of his eye and before I knew what was happening both dogs were off and running across the grass, coming after us. But by now I knew the best thing for me to do. I just kept right on walking, and left the dog diplomacy to Buck.

From way out in the desert I could see the Wasatch Mountain Range. Though it was still 70 miles away, the sun was reflecting brilliantly off two years of unusually heavy snowfall. Just watching those mountains get closer did a lot to relieve the monotony of a continually bleak winter.

Besides being a land of dogs, America is made of small towns, and Delta was yet another of those small desert communities, about the size of Goldfield. But as small as it was, it marked a major milestone for us. It was just 20 miles west of Delta that Buck and I completed our first 1,000 miles!

One birthday, five pairs of shoes, and what must have been a million sagebrush bushes behind us, less than three-fourths of our overall transcontinental journey remained. We celebrated that momentous day by eating a barbecued chicken while standing along the side of the road. But Alex promised a bona fide celebration dinner in an honest-to-goodness restaurant when we reached Provo. And to tell you the truth, the idea of being served a sit-down restaurant dinner with perhaps even a white linen napkin was very appealing to me.

As we walked down Delta's main street, Buck, in his excitement, ran through the open door of a barbershop. I was half a block away when I heard a man yell at the top of his lungs, "Get that dog outta here!" And frankly I can't say that I blamed him. The barber had a customer tipped back in a chair with a white cloth draped over his chest and an open razor in his hand over the client's neck. That was not the time for a large Doberman to start trying to make new friends.

Provo, 40 miles south of Salt Lake City, lies almost mid-point between Denver and San Francisco. Compared to Delta and the string of one-café towns we'd been through, it would seem enormous to us, although the population of Provo could fit more than nine times into a city the size of San Francisco. Provo is a college town, home of Brigham Young University, and I bet that it would be big enough to have a full-fledged white-napkined restaurant.

As Buck and I continued on Highway 6, hurrying along to Provo, we came upon some curious dome-shaped stone ovens, several stories high. They looked like those ceramic beehive-shaped containers filled with honey that are sold in some speciality stores. I knew, of course, that the West had developed when valuable ores were found in the hills. I presumed that those beehive ovens had been used to make the charcoal for melting down the ore. As though to confirm my observations, my map showed the location of a town named Miners-ville, just south of where we stood, on the banks of the Beaver River close to Wildcat Wash. I was poking around in the shadows inside those empty kilns when I heard the lonesome wail of a locomotive whistle. I stepped back outside into the sun in time to see an engine pulling a string of gondolas loaded with sugar beets, winding around a curve. And something about that train in the lonesome valley, behind the charcoal kilns, made me feel more "out West" than I ever had before.

Utah is as different from its neighbor to the west as any state can be. Even though the first permanent settlement in Nevada had been made by Mormons, I saw very little of their influence there, whereas in Utah their presence was felt in many positive ways. Utahns call their state the Beehive State, which made coming upon those beehive kilns seem especially appropriate to me. The organization and activity typical of a colony of bees is certainly evident here. Utahns are efficient, hospitable, churchgoing people. And during the six weeks that it took us to walk the 355 miles across the state, I never saw so many families participating together, nor so many happy, healthy children looking absolutely spick-and-span.

We were in the same wide-open desert landscape that we'd been in for many weeks, but now that we were over the Utah border, the rubbish that had cluttered the Nevada roadsides had all but disappeared. Here we walked litter-free roads connecting organized, well-scrubbed communities, and that cleanliness penetrated to the corners of the state. This was Mormon country.

For years I'd lived only one state removed from Utah, but what did I know about Mormons? Not very much. I knew that at one time they had practiced polygamy, but had given up the practice of multiple wives in order to have the benefits of becoming the forty-fifth state. The seclusion they'd sought by coming way out here, beyond what was then the frontier of the day, was lost forever when the gold seekers came running over their hills. There are those still religiously committed to having a number of wives and a multitude of children, but they seem to have crossed over the southern border to Arizona, which leaves them alone.

As we got closer to Provo, I saw signs of flooding that would mark our journey throughout Utah. Two years' accumulation of snowfall was still on the mountains, and the sun was melting it fast. Water plunged out of the hills, rivers burst their banks, and everywhere I saw men running to throw sandbags along the banks of waterways in an effort to control the rising waters. Even the Great Salt Lake, that wide body of water that is so salty that swimmers can't sink in it, was beginning to overflow. I heard more than one report that the streets of Salt Lake City, 20 miles from the lake, were already flooding.

But the very conditions that caused the emergency also created landscapes of breathtaking beauty. Lakes and streams shimmered in the reflection of a springtime sky. Wildflowers opened and danced in the fields. Buck ran onto the surface of Mona Reservoir. He thought the light green pollen that had collected on the surface was an extension of the meadow and went under, taking a sudden dunking. He dragged himself out of the lake and shook off the water the best that he could, but he wore a strange coating of green until the wind dried him off and blew away the pollen.

Spring was here! I could tell if for no other reason than that Buck was eating grass again. Sometimes it seemed that the amount he consumed rivaled that of a goat! Now that we were closing in on the mountains, we were surrounded at last by vast meadows of grass.

Provo lies at the foot of the western side of the Wasatch Range. And the water pouring out of those hills was rolling right through town. Mostly it stayed within the creeks braced with sandbags. Yet many of the roads we walked into town had water so deep that it ran over the tops of my sneakers.

Because of the imminent danger of more serious flooding, we decided to put Home Sweet Home in a private campground just north of town. I felt a lot better knowing that the grounds were patrolled at night and that if an overall emergency evacuation was called, we would be awakened in time. Nevertheless, we slept in our clothes, and we did not do the housecleaning and setting out of things that we normally did. We had found out early in the trip that while traveling down the road, anything not securely fastened down ended up on the floor. So we stayed ready to move at moment's notice by leaving the computer, books, maps, and pots and pans on the floor. As we stepped awkwardly over these possessions, Buck sometimes ran right into them in his confusion at the change of routine.

On May 10 Buck and I walked north out of Provo and turned east into the canyon that would take us over the rugged Uintah Mountains. The canyon walls closed us in and narrowed the road. We walked beside a string of cars that were stopped with their motors idling. It seemed quite normal by now to converse with Buck, so I told him, "Uh-oh, Buck, looks like the canyon is closed." Buck always tries hard to know what I mean. He does it by tilting his head to one side and lifting his ears, which look more like flaps, and he gets two little narrow furrows between his brows from the effort. "C'mon, Buck, let's go on anyway." No one stopped us. We passed the cars and came to a traffic controller standing like a sentry in the middle of the road. She was wearing a flame orange vest and her hair curled over the rim of her hard hat. She rotated a sign on a pole at intervals: SLOW, it said on one side, STOP on the other.

I was frankly surprised to see a young woman doing that job in Utah, because the Mormon church takes an active role in educating its members on family responsibilities that follow very traditional lines. Men support the families, women support the home. I noticed fewer women working outside the home here than in other states we went through. But where they do, it's impressive the way they get things done.

Before we left California, I'd opened a checking and savings account in a bank that advertised interstate service. "Just what we needed," I'd thought. Well, it wasn't until we were out of California that I found out that the service wasn't yet in effect. So thereafter, getting even the simplest banking procedures done by mail became a long-distance nightmare. Checks got lost and were never found; deposits either weren't received or sometimes took forever to clear. That is, until we came to Utah, where it seems banking transactions are handled for the most part by women, at least at the lower level. While in Utah, when we cashed checks, wired money, or whatever, transactions were handled with unbelievable accuracy and simple old-fashioned courtesy. But when we left, banking became confused again.

Buck and I had walked all morning in the canyon and still no one had stopped us, until we rounded a bend in the road and came upon some heavy equipment. Giant bulldozers were scooping up massive boulders and dropping them with a bone-crushing thud into huge pickup trucks. As I listened I heard the deafening rumble of more equipment from farther up the canyon, and periodically an ear-shattering blast vibrated the canyon walls. The sun was hot and directly overhead and the air motionless. Monoxide fumes and blasting dust mixed with the jarring noise, all of it hanging heavy in the air.

The harsh metallic grating was becoming alarmingly loud when we rounded a curve and I was astounded to see what looked like a massive full-fledged factory located at the side of the road. I was fascinated by the amount and variety of equipment, all rattling and cranking at once. So Buck and I struggled to climb up the side of a huge pile of crushed rock to get a better view. But the rock kept slipping away from under our feet, so I sat down, pressing back into it, and watched the enormous mechanized equipment mash, grind, pulverize, convey, dump, lift, and pile boulders into gravel of various grades and size. The mountain was being chewed up, spewed out, and transformed into material for widening the road. I was relaxing, leaning back against the rock fragments with my arms behind my head, when I glanced up and apparently just in time. Directly above us a dump truck spilled its load and an avalanche of rock started rolling down the hill. I grabbed Buck by the collar and jumped out of the way, just in time to escape being buried under tons of pea-sized gravel!

It took me longer to scrub up that night. It seemed that no amount of soap and water would get rid of that mountain canyon grime.

But Alex had found a restaurant for the thousand-mile celebration. This was the occasion to wear the one special dress, a beautiful raspberry red challis, that I had brought along. I poked around in the overhead cabinets looking for my shoes. But after searching the camper, which didn't take very long, I came to the conclusion that they must have been left behind. So I wore the best that I had. It was a toss-up between a newer pair of heavy-duty gray jogging shoes, splattered with a little mud, and a pair of yellow rubber thongs. I opted for the thongs.

The restaurant was wonderful. It was a small, intimate one with a candle and a rose on every table, and, you bet, the white linen napkin! This was no roadside café.

"Would you like to celebrate with a glass of wine with your dinner?" Alex asked.

"Sure, let's toast the first 1,000 miles and salute the second thousand, too."

A young woman came to our table to take our order, and Alex said, in his deeply timbred French accent, "Would you please bring us two glasses of Chablis?"

"I'm sorry, sir, I cannot serve you." That was a surprise, as we had read in a tourist brochure that Utah is not a dry state.

A man came quickly to our table and said, *"Pardon, monsieur, parlez-vous français?"*

"Bien sûr," Alex replied, and René, who was the owner, explained in French the restrictions that regulate the serving of liquor.

"Utah was a dry state," he said, "because Mormons don't drink. But the law was changed so as to not discourage tourists. Liquor is sold now, but only in a very few restaurants and is regulated by the state."

Therefore, to have a glass of wine, Alex was requested to walk across the room to a counter set in full public view. There he was asked to sign his name before he could purchase a split, which is half a bottle of wine, as wine may not be sold by the glass. Neither may anyone carry the wine to your table for you or pull the cork. And it was quite apparent why. As Mormons don't drink, what Mormon in good standing would be seen doing that? And yet, while having dinner, we noticed a party of four. The gentleman who appeared to be the host, after cautiously surveying the room, lowered one glass tumbler at a time under the table where a brown bag was concealed.

Two days later I was invited to speak with students in the upper grades in an elementary school in Orem, a few miles north of Provo. I was still a block away from the school when I saw the youngsters crossing a lawn, walking from their school to the gymnasium, each carrying a chair. When they saw me coming, they waved. Inside the gym they arranged their chairs in rows and started asking questions.

"Are you going to walk back, too?" asked a girl who wore her incredulity upon her face.

"No," I said, laughing, "I'm going to leave that for you to do."

And then I got this one. It came from a serious young man, one of the few who wasn't blond. His name was Dave, he told me, and he was eleven. Dave seemed so confident I wondered why he asked the question he did. "What do you do about rejection?" he said, and he really wanted to know. I knew well enough what he was asking. I was only one year older than Dave when I was laughed off a stage.

It happened when I was a new student in a large junior high school in San Francisco. One day I used my ten-minute break between classes to sit down at the piano in the school auditorium so the student-body president could hear me play. "Would you do that for the assembly on Friday?" he said.

I agreed. I loved to play and I was accustomed to being before an audience. On Friday I walked onto the stage and sat down. I had no music. I didn't need it. I placed my fingers on the keys and began. But just as I was starting the third movement, something happened that has never happened to me before. For an instant—and that's all it took—I forgot my rapport with Tchaikovsky and focused instead on the audience. What are they thinking of me? I wondered, for I had developed a self-consciousness that was new to me then. I froze. I forgot everything. I forgot the music, what my fingers were doing, everything. Then I panicked, which made matters even worse.

Somehow I managed to collect my wits and began again, starting at the beginning. But I was so nervous that it might happen again that it did! I got to the same spot in the music and forgot everything. This time I got up from the bench and walked off the stage. The audience giggled and laughed and tittered, and something inside me withered. At that moment I made a somber decision: "I will never put myself in front of an audience again." That day, I remember, I went home to an empty house and had no one with whom I could share my failure.

For twelve years I suppressed that experience. When it tried to emerge, I was quick to shut it down, putting a secure lid on it. I changed my thinking so that I wouldn't experience the pain again, for every time I recalled it for even an instant I was overwhelmed with shame. It was many years before I could think about it and simply consider it for what it was, without adding the feelings that had always come up in response to the memory of that incident. I could just look at the incident and choose to feel another way about it, and I did.

I didn't want to tell Dave all that. But he had asked about rejection, so I told the children a story about Buck instead.

"Dave, when Buck meets up with another dog, he always shows interest and waits to see if the other dog does, too. Does the dog just want to play? That's what Buck wants to know. Because some dogs, you know, like some people, have learned to be defensive and Buck wants to know that in advance.

"Well, one day, Buck met a beauty. A shepherd came down his driveway waving a tail like a plume high up over his back. Buck trotted forward eagerly, stopped, then taking that wagging tail for an invitation, he ran the remaining few steps.

"In just seconds that dog had Buck on the ground and his teeth were at his throat. Buck rolled away and up onto his feet, and if a dog can look surprised, Buck surely did.

"He shook himself off, took a last look, and trotted off again. And I watched to see what he'd do. Did he feel rejected? No, Dave, he didn't. Did he feel bad? No. As a matter of fact, he didn't seem to change his opinion about himself at all. The other dog didn't want to play. That's all. Buck would find one who did.

"Well, it seems to me that Buck has the right idea about rejection. We can put hurt feelings to an experience, if that's what we want to do. I can feel bad, or hurt, or happy, or sad, but *I'm the one who adds the feeling.*"

I sure thought I knew what I was saying when I was talking with those kids. But I took Dave's question back into the canyon and gnawed on it like Buck does on a bone. "We add our own feelings to an experience," I heard myself saying, and then it hit me like a ton of bricks. If that's true, then I'm the one who's adding fear to my experience of height. And once I got that, I was only a hair's breadth away from an obvious conclusion. If that's true, that I add the fear, then why don't I replace it? I knew when I made the decision to walk across America that my fear of heights would be a problem for me, but I wanted to make the trip anyway. I also knew that fear normally wouldn't stop me. I could be afraid and still do what I wanted to do. Nevertheless, along the way I always looked hard at my map to see in advance where the high places I'd come to would be. That way I could steel myself against them and not be taken by surprise. And when I'd see a highway sign announcing a bridge coming up ahead, the fear would begin crawling over my scalp and I'd wonder, How high can it be? and How long? Even before we got up to a height I would start the gut-wringing, armpit-drenching dread and anticipation. And when I got right up to the bridge, I'd stand there awhile and measure its length with my eyes, calculating how long it would take to walk the first half, because I'd think to myself, if I can walk the first half of that bridge, then I probably can do the last. And then I would take it ten feet at a time, or five, whatever I was up to that day, though the sweat on the brow would accompany every step.

Give up my fear of height? You mean instead of fearing height, I could learn to enjoy it? Was that possible? I had tried in the past to push the fear down, to repress it. I'd even taken flying lessons to try to overcome it. I'd learned to fly the plane, all right, but not to give up the reeling, the spots before my eyes, the light-headed misery. A fifty-three-year habit. Could I really replace it? I was afraid to try.

But for well over four months now I had been out in the wilderness where the only intrusion into that natural world was the road that we were walking. For months I had been enclosed in a tranquil world that nurtures, and it just was not possible to spend that much time with what nature has to share and to remain the same. Nor was it possible to handle the situations that came up on the road, more often than I could ever have believed was possible, without also going beyond what once had seemed important. As a result, I was growing in a way that staying at home could never have accomplished. I'd been a fear-of-height cageling far too long. Give up my fear of height? I simply had to try.

Things have a way of presenting themselves, it seems, just when you are ready. I already knew what I wanted to do when we came upon a sign that was surely destined to be there. "The World's Steepest Aerial Tramway" was just up ahead and scheduled to open for the season on the day that we would pass it. I didn't tell Alex in advance what I wanted to do. I waited until the last minute. That gave me a bit of hedge in case I got cold feet and wanted to change my mind. If I let Alex know, he would want me to succeed, and I didn't want to complicate my own emotions with expectancies of his.

I had no lingering doubts that any fear I had about height was what I continued to put there. After all, I had reasoned, if there were anything inherent in height itself, it would produce in all of us the same reaction. And clearly that isn't so. Alex isn't afraid of height, and neither are many others. It was that simple. I had added fear to my experience, and it didn't matter why.

So, on April 10 I stood on the passengers' platform with my tramway ticket and sweating palms. Alex was silently supportive beside me. I'd asked him not even to talk to me. I wanted to be free from distractions. I watched a gondola swing by a cable, slowly inching upward. It sure was steep; that blue and gray gondola was already looking small. I felt the shirt under my arms growing wet when an empty gondola swung onto the platform and stopped in front of me. I pulled back. I wasn't ready. This was happening too fast for me. I let the couple just behind me get into the empty car and it swung off and began to climb. Just watching them made my head begin to swim and I rigidly held my breath.

"Elena," I said to myself, "remember, you are the one who says how it is. Let go of your fear. You no longer have to have it." And I began to teach myself another way to view it. I drew air back into my lungs, relaxed the tension I was holding in my body, and found that I could let the feeling of fear slip away along with my breath. And I reminded myself continuously: Let it go, let it drift away, don't hang on to it. And I felt the tension I was gripping with muscle strength dissolve.

That first success was all I needed to know that I *could* do it. But the habit of feeling the surge of panic and then pulling it in was so engrained that it automatically came into play. I stayed alert, very aware of what I wanted to accomplish. Every time I noticed terror start to control me, I reminded myself again to relax, let go of the tension. And I remembered to breathe, gently, oh so gently. I did it over and over again. Breathe gently and relax. Breathe gently and relax.

Another tram swung into place and now there was nobody else behind me. This was it. Alex and I stepped in and I felt the cage sway under my feet. The door slammed with a bang that vibrated the metal walls, and with a jolt we were off and climbing. The cabin swung violently from the sudden start as we started over the river and began the almost vertical 1,700-

foot climb to an overhanging cliff. My heart beat wildly; there was no escape. My hand was locked in a white-knuckle grip on the rails across the windows.

What if I can't stand it? I no longer have a choice. The door had closed; we were clicking along. There's no other way. I can't get out. I'll be caged till the final round.

Maybe, I thought, if I scream and beat on the cabin wall, or hang on the side and make a hysterical riot, the operator will back up the tram and Alex will get me out.

But through the mindless commotion, another thought came through: Elena, is that what you want to do? I loosened my grip on the bars and eased the pounding in my chest by slowing down my breathing. And I looked at what I was seeing, and it wasn't so bad, after all.

Our open cabin jerked along the cable. It swung over the white-water river dashing wildly over giant boulders below. The wind howled up the canyon, rocking us about, while all the time we were lifting closer to the face of the gray sedimentary rock, climbing up the wall.

A descending gondola slid past us, I looked down on its roof and was listening to the wind whine on the overhead cable when we came to a sudden stop. The door slammed open and I stepped out onto the canyon cliff, reminding myself to breathe, and walked, though just a bit slowly, over to the rail. The river, hundreds of yards below, was a smooth silvery ribbon, the road and the thin dark strip of the railroad tracks paralleling its path. Over on the right, the beautiful double cataract of Bridal Veil Falls spilled over the edge of a cliff, and a rainbow arched in the misty curtain that covered the canyon wall.

Alex stepped up beside me and broke his promise of silence. He could tell by my composure it would be all right. He took my hand and confirmed his pride. "You really were able to do it."

When I had stayed as long as I wanted and the tram was ready to return, we stepped back into the cabin and began our descent to the valley. But fate had one more trick to play. Alex was taking pictures through the open cabin window. But he had not relaxed. He couldn't be absolutely certain of my new reactions, and he didn't know when he might have to step in and try to assist me. As though to make my experience totally complete, we came to a jerking halt that threw the gondola into a lurch like a pendulum out of control. When Alex saw an attendant below run from the gondola platform to the building that housed the mechanical operation, it was he who almost panicked.

What could be wrong? Alex didn't dare to look at me. He didn't know what he'd find. Maybe this will be too much for her, he thought; maybe she'll lose control. But what could he do if I did? He held his breath, pretending to take more pictures, but I saw him turn his head, ever so slightly, to see what I was doing. But I was ready for him. With a grin on my face I jerked up my thumb to let him know I was okay. Whatever it was that had caused the delay didn't take long to fix and soon we were on our way again, descending to the platform. Now I knew better than ever that habits once learned don't have to remain in place.

Buck and I were heading for Heber, still ten miles away. At Heber we would take a sharp right onto Highway 40 and continue up Daniels Canyon to Strawberry Reservoir, where we'd next locate Home Sweet Home. And a more perfect spot would be hard to find. There we looked out on a lake as clear and blue as a baby's eyes. The conifers wore a cover of snow, and an occasional jay landing on a branch shook the powder free. The silence was as pure as it ever gets.

But still in the canyon the Wasatch National Forest surrounded us with the sweet smell of sun-warmed earth. Great stands of pine covered the canyon walls, and leaves on the aspen trees trembled delicately in the gentlest breeze. Water poured from the mountainside and every now and again Buck and I were startled when water-sodden earth broke loose from the side of the hill and spilled across the road.

We made a turn in the road and surprised a group of mule deer. They stood for a few moments twitching their ears assessing the danger we presented. Apparently none, as they took the time to stare a few moments before moving silently back to the forest.

Just east of Heber City I stopped a few moments to look back. Off in the west a dark gray sky was forming. I didn't give it much attention, although I tried to determine which way it was heading. Most of the storms there come rolling in from the west, but this one was still far away and I couldn't tell in which direction it was blowing.

I heard the first clap of thunder when we were about three miles out of Heber. I turned again and was surprised to see that the clouds had come up behind us so fast. The sky was rapidly growing darker and a bolt of lightning flashed across the landscape. Then the first drops of water began to sprinkle on the ground and another clap of thunder louder than the first rolled across the sky. As far as I could see ahead, the road was bound on both sides by fenced pasture, in which a few trees had been left, although they were way back on a rocky hill. Even if I jumped the fence, I knew better than to take refuge under a tree. Lightning will strike the highest point, making those trees the very worst place to be. Once I'd read that more people are killed in electrical storms than in any other natural disaster. That made me hurry along faster with my head bent low and my hood pulled over my hair, although there was nothing in the way of shelter for us to hurry to. The storm was all around us now, dark, threatening, and violent. Those lightning bolts threw voltage around with a thunderous roar as though Thor were working the sky.

About a mile ahead I saw a car parked on the side of the road. I hurried even more, because I had remembered that a car is as good as anyplace to be in an electrical storm—something about the tires acting as insulation. As it was now,

Buck and I were the highest things around and therefore likely targets to conduct electrical current back into the ground.

We were getting closer to that car when I was alarmed to see the ground move in front of me. As a matter of fact, the motion startled me so much that I was ready to doubt my eyes when I saw it move again. I stopped to get my bearings, to try to make sense of this impossible sight, and watched a disk of ground rise up in the air. Only it wasn't a piece of ground but a manhole cover, and an arm was lifting it up. That was just about the last thing I could expect out here. And when I was almost upon it, I saw a man down in the hole, with the metal plate upon his hands. He was as startled to see me as I'd been to find him. Nevertheless, I badly wanted shelter, so I stood there in the rain, the electricity shattering the air, and called down to the man standing in the hole. "Excuse me, but is that your car over there?" I yelled as politely as I could.

"Yes, ma'am," he yelled back.

All I could see was his shadowed face, but his voice was gentle and kind. "Would you mind terribly if we took shelter in it until the storm blows over?"

"I'd sure like to let you"—he was really apologetic—"but I'm already late—this storm you know—and I've got to be moving on." He climbed out of the hole and dropped the cover in place.

"What do people do," I asked, clutching at straws for some good advice, "when they get caught in storms around here?"

"Just pray, lady. Best thing to do is just pray."

The storm lasted longer than I liked, but as frequently happens in the mountains, it blew over fast, the sun came out, and almost before we knew it Buck and I were dry.

But the newly dampened earth brought out earth and animal scents that sent Buck tearing over the hills, trying to gather them all in at once. I saw him running down the side of the mountain, carrying something in his mouth. It was hard to tell just what it was, most likely the remains of a fox. Anyway, it was wet and dead, about half the size of Buck. All

that was left of the poor creature was its mud-specked baggy
skin, and as Buck ran with the carcass, it flapped behind him
in the wind and clouds of hair flew off. He dropped it at my
feet as though to share the loot, and then did something I'd
never seen him do. He dropped down onto the skin and
clumsily rolled around, acting like a silly cat playing with a
catnip mouse. But the odor of death reached my nostrils, and
though Buck was reluctant to stop, after getting in a few more
good rolls he got back onto his feet and shook off the matted
hairs. I grabbed him by the collar to drag him away from his
prize, and though he let me lead him away, he kept looking
back over his shoulder.

The sun reflected off the snow in the hills and I felt it on
my face. I took the sunscreen from my pocket that I'd bought
in Heber and smeared some on my nose, which surprisingly
was beginning to burn. But we were getting high up in the
mountains, and the thinner air, combined with the snow's
reflection, was beginning to take effect. So I began washing
my face in the morning with baby oil instead of soap, and
thereafter discovered it worked just fine—it was all the protection I'd need. Some of my friends had worried about my
getting leathery skin from weather exposure, but it didn't
happen.

While I smoothed on the lotion, I sat on the hillside to
enjoy the view of the mountains before shoving off again. I
had so much enjoyed the desert but now that I was surrounded
by the forest, I was as moved by its beauty as anyplace I'd
been. It seems that where I am is always the most beautiful
place of all.

Strawberry Reservoir marked our passage over the Wasatch
Mountains. I felt a tinge of regret at leaving the pine-covered
mountains. But we had to move on, so we relocated the
camper at Fruitland, 22 miles ahead, and Buck and I began
our journey through what my map told me would be high,

dry tableland—a plateau so arid and barren it was bad enough to give back to the Indians, which is exactly what had been done. We would continue along Highway 40, crossing the Uintah and Ouray Indian reservations and through the towns of Duchesne and Roosevelt, and then go on to Vernal. Vernal would be our last town in Utah before Colorado. But before we left the forest I saw yet another sign of the hardship caused by the heavy winter snows. The weather had driven countless deer out of the hills to lower elevations to forage for food. Some had apparently been confused by headlights from vehicles on the road. Now they were along the roadside in various states of decay. It was tragically grotesque to see their swollen bellies, their legs spread awkwardly in the air, while perfectly intact skeletons were all that remained of some. The stench was sickening, made even more so by the heat, and my stomach turned in spasms, revolted by the smell. Buck sniffed at one of those unfortunate deer but recoiled as though he sensed a danger. Then he walked gingerly around the corpses as though to avoid their fate.

Looking ahead to a town with a name like Fruitland, I was expecting an oasis on our horizon. We hadn't seen orchards since leaving California and I was hungry to see fruit ripening on trees again. But any fruit in Fruitland had to be in the refrigerators, for it certainly wasn't on the trees. There were trees, all right. I could see aspens high up in the hills, where they grew as thick as weeds. And I stopped a few minutes to watch two men rolling the roots of aspen trees in burlap sacks and then throwing them onto a truck. They were trucking them to a big city nursery, miles and miles away.

So Fruitland had obviously come by its name another way. I was told that a number of years before, some enterprising hustlers recognized a land opportunity that could turn out to be as profitable as the gold rush. They plotted off portions of these barren lands, renamed the section Fruitland, took pictures of native junipers, and called those stubby pine shrubs fruit trees. Maybe those pictures were a bit out of focus, because those parcels sold off like hotcakes to speculating easterners craving a bit of the old, wild West.

Even before we reached Fruitland, while still coming down from the hills, I saw Buck take one of his shortcuts, which seemed always to turn out long. He cut through a dry ravine, probably looking for water, when he came upon and startled a full-grown mountain sheep. The ewe was walking the narrowest trail and had two little lambs in tow. I called to Buck in a muffled voice to come and stand by my side. We stayed that way quietly, to give her a chance to move on.

She panicked instead, showing her terror in the wild roll of her eyes. She voiced an alarm to the two little ones behind. But the trail ran up against a vertical wall, where the three of them huddled. She couldn't go forward, nor could she move backward, for when she tried, the lambs crowded around her legs, blocking her way from behind and bunching up even closer.

I was weighing how I might help her when from high up the canyon wall we heard the sound of bleating, a clear commanding call. And there, on the rim of the canyon, stood a large, magnificent ram surveying the scene with composure. The ewe heard his call and looked up to the cliff, and he bleated to her again. When she tried to move, the lambs stumbled about to get closer to their mom.

He was insistent and his message filled the canyon. He kept it up and that cut through her confusion. She took a few steps backward, pushing the lambs along, and continued stumbling back until she came to a place on the trail wide enough to turn around.

She was elevated above us on that trail, but she still had to pass us by. The ram kept up his persuasion until she finally dared to do it, the little ones prancing behind. They came to a place on the wall where the slope shelved moderately. It allowed her to jump from ledge to ledge, and the lambs, in smaller leaps, bounced along behind. The ram kept calling his message until she and the two were safe. Then he took a last look down the mountain at us before he followed them over the wall.

East of Fruitland, near Starvation Lake, the earth is sun-scorched. A few scrubby plants barely survive on this wind-whipped land. It is the reservation of the Uintah and Ouray Indian nations. A century ago these Indians were nomadic people following the seasonal cycles, moving into the valleys in winter and to the mountains in summer. They no longer have that option, for they are confined to a smaller land. But what an irony I discovered here. Under the surface of that barren land, unexpected deposits of oil and shale were found. As a result, by leasing their lands to development companies interested in the underground reserves, some of these reserva-tion Indians are rich beyond the wildest white man's dreams.

I talked with Ute tribal leaders working to lead their people into the modern world. When Alex was asked to talk with a group of Indian students about computers, he accepted with alacrity. A combination of thirty years of international associ-ation with computers and a compassion he wears on his sleeve makes his talks with youngsters about computers vividly inter-esting and easy for them to understand.

Here in the high country tableland, the red earth is scored with sharp-sided arroyas, ravines so steep that any rain making it over the Wasatch peaks doesn't hang around for very long. Drinking water was scarce. That was a problem, especially for Buck, who continued to chase everything in sight and as a result always worked up a whopping thirst. I could spot watering holes from a distance even better than Buck, simply because I was taller and usually up on the road, which was raised above the ground.

To make certain Buck didn't miss those opportunities, I sharpened my whistle. A short tone ending on a higher pitch always brought him running. Then I'd point with my finger or the stick, and Buck knew just what that meant. He'd start off with the speed of a jackrabbit, his nose close to the ground, and then take his fill while lying in the water, cooling himself that way.

Now Buck was hot and thirsty. I could tell because he was scouting every gully, sniffing at empty bottles, but he was out of luck; there was no water here. The canteen I'd strapped to my belt had been emptied hours before. We would be coming to Antelope Creek, however. It couldn't be far ahead.

Buck found it before I did. He heard the roar of the water and suddenly took off, running straight ahead. I saw him run down an embankment, then I heard a splash and water sprayed up in the air.

I ran to see what had happened. The sodden earth on the riverbank had crumbled beneath his weight and the water was dark and muddy where Buck had disappeared. I scanned the swirling water rushing at furious speed, fully expecting to see Buck staunchly swimming to join me on the shore. But Buck was gone, snatched by the force of the river, so all I saw was churning white water, funneling under a bridge.

The river was swollen and ugly where it came down to meet the bridge, and had carried along its furious path branches and logs scoured from the countryside. The water level was dangerously high because of the melting snow and was but a scant few inches from the bottom of the bridge, where a mountain of debris, jammed like a dam, wedged against the bridge.

I ran up onto the bridge which shuddered from the force of the current exploding underneath, and searched downstream, looking as far as I could, but all I saw was the pounding rush of a rampaging swollen stream.

Then I heard Buck's yelp of pain coming from under the bridge. How could that possibly be? The force of the water was swift and strong. I couldn't see how Buck could be treading there. He had to be caught in the tangle of brush that had snagged and gathered there. Buck was alive, but he was under the bridge, with mere inches of air to spare.

An experience like this happens too fast to give you time to think about what to do. My mind accelerated a plan on its own as reason left my head. It was unrealistic and totally reckless, suicide, to enter that water, but Buck was alive, so at least I had to try. I'd let myself down over the side, hang on to tangled branches, go arm over arm under the bridge before it was too late.

The plan was made in seconds and my shoes were already off and I had one hand on the railing when I heard an anguished yelp. Then Buck shot out of the rapids, and as quickly as he had appeared he was carried off downstream. I watched him struggle against the current, fighting to stay alive, but he was tumbled and tossed about like a twig and battered against the rocks.

Moments later, far down the stream where the river makes a bend, I saw a pitiful figure struggle to climb onto the bank. Buck didn't run to meet me. Instead, he lay on the ground. So I fought my way through the underbrush that grew along the bank, not caring at all that I wore no shoes and was bruising my stockinged feet. He had been roughed up by the raging river and his body was battered and scraped. He lifted his head to greet me and I saw he was badly hurt. I sat down on the bank beside him and started feeling his joints. He was badly bruised but he had no broken bones.

It wasn't long, however, before Buck got back on his feet. And he followed along behind me as we made our way up to the road, although I stopped every few yards and waited as he limped along.

That night I brought out the miracle bag balm and rubbed it on his wounds. The next day I didn't have the heart to go off on the road without him, so we spent the day in the camper and caught up on our fan mail instead.

EIGHT

·····••••··••·•••··•••··••••··•

On the Top of It

For weeks on end Buck and I had been out in areas so remote that getting hold of a newspaper was frequently out of the question. Even in those communities large enough to support a monthly publication, the news was very local. In those papers someone's cow straying from its pasture could and did sometimes make front-page copy. And so, while we were out in that hinterland, events had been going on of which I knew very little.

Walking through Vernal, Utah, I began to feel the fervor that was building across the land. While we were traveling the roads of America going west to east, the Olympic torch relay started its course, going east to west, and someplace along Highway 40 we were destined to meet. In 1984 the nation was still caught up in the depressing grip of the dishearteningly long economic recession, but the Olympic runner was coming, and that was something to get excited about. He wasn't due in Vernal for another three weeks, but already I felt the beat. Here was a reason for Vernal residents to pull out the stops, polish the brass, get ready to show the runner the best they had to offer. Flags began to flutter on spacious front verandas, and the five-ring Olympic symbol was displayed in store windows and on car bumpers. There was a stirring of good old-fashioned national pride, and the very best part of all the excitement was that the heady, charged-up, united effort wasn't one for war.

It was not quite time to cheer on the runners. For now, the biggest attraction in Vernal was the dinosaurs. Just twenty miles east of town, the bones of fossilized prehistoric beasts are exposed in a slab of the mountain, right before your eyes. Back in town, Buck and I had passed along the iron-fenced Dinosaur Gardens, where life-sized replicas of dinosaurs and reptiles stand. Buck had taken a defensive stance when he first saw them through the bars. As we walked by, an attendant came out of the museum. I called out to her, "Do you allow dogs in there?" although I fully expected her to decline.

She answered, "No, we don't." But Buck has winning ways. The attendant hesitated, her eyes on him. "We're really not that busy," she said. "Why don't you come on in."

I led Buck past the glass display cases in which fragments of bones were on view. A few visitors turned their heads with astonishment when they saw the red-haired dog quietly padding by. Soon we passed outside to the gardens, where Buck stopped dead in his tracks. He looked up at the brontosaurus and woolly mammoth and lowered himself to the ground, then he stealthily crept up closer, but the beasts didn't move and it was only seconds before Buck realized that they weren't alive. Then, raising himself up to full stature, with conspicuous indifference, he turned and saluted the beasts with a careless toss of his leg.

On June 10 Buck and I stepped over the Utah-Colorado state line and into the middle of Dinosaur, a border town. Dinosaur was as close to a ghost town as I ever saw, with only a few bars, their doors swinging desolately on a single hinge, and a couple of motels. Most everything else was closed and barred up. By the looks of it, Dinosaur had seen better days.

Still, even here I felt it: the Olympic torch was coming and Dinosaur was doing its part.

"Hi! Getting ready for the big event?" I called out to a man in paint-splattered coveralls standing in front of a midsize replica of a *Tyrannosaurus rex*. He held a trowel of plaster in his hand and was daubing at holes in the dinosaur's carcass. A bucket of paint was nearby ready to finish the job of swabbing the beast in celebratory pink.

"You bet! Not every day we have somethin' like this. This is somethin' to tell the grandkids!"

With a wave of the hand we continued on. It was blistering hot, and after crossing Cliff Creek, Buck had little groundwater to drink. The prairie dogs were driving him crazy again. "Chi! chi! chi! chi! chi!" Buck vaulted after them. But as usual they disappeared just as Buck closed in, leaving him frustrated and digging in their holes.

This hide-and-seek routine had been going on all day and Buck was dragging way behind. I was well ahead of him when I noticed a skunk meandering daintily across the road. It moved at a leisurely pace and I stopped to watch the lovely creature, thinking, "I'm sure glad that Buck isn't with me," when I heard thumpity-thumpity-thump closing the distance between us. "No! Stop, Buck. Don't do it!" It was too late. He cut the skunk off at the side of the road, where it turned tail and let fly with its instinct, giving it to Buck full in the face.

Buck cried out, his lips ran with saliva, and his eyes watered. He rubbed at his face over and over with his paws but it didn't help. The stench was overwhelming. It burned my eyes, making it hard to breathe, and though I tried, there was no getting away from the noxious scent surrounding him. The only thing we had going for us was the downhill wind, so I covered my nose and pushed on up the hill.

We hadn't gone far when I saw an elderly townsman sitting in the shade of an old wooden front stoop, rocking on the back legs of a caned chair. I sure didn't know what to do with Buck, but I figured that a native might know. "Hello," I called from a distance. "My dog had a run-in with a skunk. Can you tell me what to do?"

He pulled an old gray felt hat down lower on his brows, then spat in the dust before answering. "Tomato juice. Vinegar'll do the same," he said, squeezing his eyes together to look at nothing far up the road.

"Both work as well?"

"Use what you got. Dog don't care."

I stopped at the local store and bought a bottle of vinegar. I was barely able to stand getting close to him, and to make matters worse, Buck flung the vinegar off as fast as I poured it on. Still I managed to work some of the vinegar into his hair down to the skin, over his muzzle, around his eyes, and into his ears. For the most part, the vinegar did the job. But even two months later, when Buck got too close, you could still tell what had happened.

From Vernal, Utah, to Craig, Colorado, is an uphill climb of 123 miles. In that stretch of the road our maps showed that we would pass through places with names like Skull Creek, Cross Mountains, and Elk Springs. But just try to find them! Somewhere on that high mountain plateau, Alex was looking for a place to put the camper. Elk Springs was roughly midpoint and therefore an obvious location, but he had passed it by a couple of times and had to backtrack again to find it. Eventually he came back to tell me about it.

"In Elk Springs there's a lady named Ruth who runs a motel and café and can put us up. It's perfect. There's a well for water, and electricity we can plug into the camper. You are really going to love it."

"How much farther?" Alex handed me a jug of water from the trunk and poured some into a plastic tub for Bucky. I tipped the jug and let about half a quart of the sun-heated water gurgle down my throat. Buck was lying in the shade under the car. His paws straddled the bowl and he slurped noisily, his chin resting in the water. Crickets jumped around him, some bouncing off his body, but he was tired and paid no attention to them.

Perspiration was dripping off my face and rivulets of moisture trickled into the small of my back.

"About eight more miles. Are you okay?" Alex asked. "If you are, I'll go ahead and have everything ready when you get there."

"Sure, we're fine." I said, looking forward to a shower.

About two and a half hours later I saw Home Sweet Home blocking the entrance to Ruth's Café. Out at the edge of the road, a sign swiveled on a rusty iron frame, "Good Food, Stop Here." The parking lot was immense, big enough to hold a fleet of trucks, but except for the camper, it was completely empty.

On the porch, next to an ice machine, a woman with a scarf wrapped peasant style around her head and a large dish towel tied around her waist teetered precariously on a rickety wooden chair. Ruth was hanging on to the back of the chair while reaching up above her head, trying to plug a heavy black extension cord into a porcelain socket in the ceiling. The chair wobbled under her. "Is it working?" she yelled over her shoulder.

"No," Alex yelled back from inside the R.V.

Ruth rattled the cord vigorously and sparks flew from the socket and a puff of smoke curled upward. "Now?"

"No."

"No problem." She snapped the cord from the socket, pulled it through the door across the room and plugged it into the wall behind the pinball machine.

I was hot, dirty, tired, and thirsty. I was also starving. I picked up a yellowed plastic folder and started reading the handwritten menu.

Ruth saw me. "You're hungry!" And it certainly wasn't a question. "I could fix you up somethin'." She looked from one of us to the other. It was evident how eager she was to treat us well. "Ever had elk? Got just a little in the freezer. Got him out back last winter." Her face cajoled us with a smile. "I could fix you up some nice elk steaks and a pot of fresh green beans. Stir up a batch of biscuits and homemade noodles, and make a lemon meringue pie for dessert." Her face was animated with the thought of the meal she was planning and didn't wait for an answer. "About six-thirty? Give me time to pick up some things." Later we realized that would be in Maybell, 24 miles away.

It sounded wonderful. "You bet!" We kicked the cord to the side of the threshold and headed for "home." We sure didn't have far to go.

The table was neatly set with two places on a blue-checked gingham cloth decorated by a pickle jar filled with wild blue lupine. The smell of garlic sizzling in a pan mixed with the sweet aroma of bacon and biscuits browning in the oven. Ruth came out of the kitchen wiping her hands on her dish-towel apron and Buck pranced through the open door when he saw her. He knew a soft touch when he saw one. Ruth patted his head while Buck licked the gravy from her spoon.

From that moment on, Buck and Ruth entered into a conspiracy. During the week we stayed there she spoiled him rotten. Each day, Buck couldn't wait to get in off the road and hit her kitchen. And I knew that if he ever got lost again, I'd know just where to look for him.

Ruth's dinner was divine. She carried two steaming plates to our table. Buck followed closely, sniffing into the air behind her. A large sizzling steak, curled at the edges, rested against a mountain of homemade egg noodles, pan gravy dripped over the top. She set down a giant bowl of garden-fresh green beans simmered with bacon, and a pile of hot buttermilk biscuits were tumbled into a plastic basket. Jellies, honey, and butter were added to the feast along with steaming hot coffee. There was food enough for six.

"You're joining us, of course," Alex invited.

"You go ahead. Eat while it's hot, and enjoy. I'll join you later."

We stabbed our forks into the feast. *"Bon appétit, mon amour,"* Alex said as he lunged into it.

When we had eaten more than we had room for, Ruth put the plates down on the floor, where Buck could benefit from the bones and the little bit of gravy that was left on them. He took a bone and holding it with his paws, began cracking it on the wooden floor. "Auntie Ruth" didn't mind at all. "Don't worry, Buck, I have plenty more for you in the kitchen. I cooked enough for you, too."

She disappeared into the kitchen and came back. "Ready for dessert?" she asked, setting down in front of us a pie piled high with thick sticky peaks of tawny meringue. She cut huge wedges from it and put them before us, the lemony filling oozing onto our plates. Believe it or not, we ended up eating the whole pie.

We had finally coaxed Ruth to join us. "Is this your place?" Alex asked.

"It's my café. I rent from the owner. I been doing good here," she said. "He'll probably be up this weekend. Gotta get in there and get them rooms cleaned up in the motel."

We were interrupted by headlights shining into the window and then a heavyset woman rushed through the open door, stepping over the cord. "Thank goodness you're still open," she gasped. "We've been driving for hours. Do you have any rooms left?"

Ruth looked at her for a moment and then, with strange indifference, turned back to the table and muttered, with her head down, "You can look at the first one, it's open." The woman was back in a minute looking bewildered. "There's no blankets in there," she said. "No pillows!"

"That's the way it is." Ruth shrugged with astonishing disregard. "Take it or leave it." The woman stood in the doorway a moment, disbelief on her face. Ruth didn't give an inch. Totally baffled, the weary traveler turned in a befuddled huff and walked back into the night.

We didn't know what to make of all that, so the silence hung heavy for a while, and then Ruth mused, "Yeah, guess I better get up there and get those rooms cleaned."

So, to restore the previous camaraderie, I spoke, making idle conversation. "You manage the motel, too, Ruth?"

"Sorta," she hedged uncomfortably, but after a moment she went on. "Look, it's something like this. Sometimes we rent rooms here. Sometimes we don't. During hunting season we mostly do. That's when I do real good. But when the owner comes and stays, he brings a pet." Another pause. And then, as though this would explain: "He shares the room with his pet."

"Yes, that's quite normal," Alex acknowledged, thinking of Buck.

"He sleeps with his pet."

"Yes," Alex replied, "some people do that."

Ruth hesitated before she went on. "His pet, you see, is a duck. The duck sleeps with him. Sometimes he fills the tub so the duck can swim. He stays in a room with that duck until he can't stand it any longer. After a while he has to move to another room. And then the next one, until they're all used up. Then he goes away and pays me to go in those rooms, strip the beds, launder the bedding, you know, clean up. Sometimes I have to use a shovel. And then"—she sighed—"he comes back again." She noticed our expression of incredulity. "So help me!"

Just then, two men in jeans came through the door, ending the conversation. Standing at the counter, one of them called out, "Two coffees," and held up two stocky fingers. Ruth made an introduction. "This here's Fred. The other, that's his son." There were now four customers in Ruth's café. Fred and Ruth represented a full two-thirds of the population of Elk Springs.

"Have a seat," Ruth called out, and with a frown of concern, "How are the crickets?"

"The problem's getting worse. They're climbing up the side of the house," Fred answered, hitching one hip onto a stool. He was dressed in dark blue jeans and a faded denim, short-sleeved shirt, stretched a little over his grandpa-sized belly, and from which the sunburned muscular arms of a farmer bulged. Now, there is something about the people from this section of the country—maybe it's the farming, being so close to the soil—whatever it is, these people are downright basic, good, and fundamental. I sensed that Fred was one of them. Right now, he had a farmer's problem. "We've got an army of them Mormon crickets marchin' through the southern acres heading for the house; they're not far now. Eatin' everything in sight." He shook his head in exasperation. "If they'd spray those things before they got this far, we wouldn't have this problem."

"Are they heading this way?" Ruth asked anxiously.

"Sure are."

"If they come this way like they did last year, I'll have to close my doors for good. Last year when them Mormon crickets left, I had no more vegetables. They stripped my garden clean."

"Last year," Ruth elaborated, "the crickets covered that parking lot out there. They were so thick folks ran over them by the millions. People would drive in and wouldn't get out of their cars. Just turn around and drive on out again."

"Why do you call them Mormon crickets?" I asked.

"Because they come out of Utah. Outta Dinosaur National Monument." I didn't mention that half of the monument lies in Colorado. "It's a national monument, you know. Can't do anything that upsets the environment. They breed over there and when they're hungry they march out of there and wipe out our fields."

"You mean, the crickets are allowed to breed on government property, the government has laws prohibiting their control on national monuments, and when the armies decide to march out of there, they descend onto private land and consume the crops and the government stands by and lets it happen?" I wanted to clarify what I was hearing.

"That's right."

"How can that be?"

"I think they don't understand how bad the problem is. We need someone to call attention to it."

"Maybe we should go see," Alex offered.

Very early the next day we jumped into Fred's red and white pickup and headed up the highway, turning onto a dirt road where you could see the wheat rippling over the horizon. A few piñon pine were on the hills and a small band of antelope leaped out of our way. The road wound its way over the hills through the wheat.

"You're looking at volunteer wheat here," Fred enlightened us. "That's wheat that comes up from last year's crops. My fields are lying fallow this year. I've fifteen hundred acres. I bought this piece of land to retire to. Has a nice house on it. But my wife, heck, she won't even come near this place now. I'll show you why. I sprayed around the house yesterday but wait till you see it."

We came around a curve and there on the crest of a hill overlooking a small valley stood the house, where we saw millions of writhing crickets, hanging on the doors, on the side of the house, clinging to the screens as close as one finger to another. As we watched, some were dying from the poison Fred had put out and were falling back onto the bodies of the ones already dead, their place taken immediately by the climbing hordes.

"My Lord, it's unbelievable!" Alex exclaimed. Off to the left, stretching across the field and advancing toward the house, was an undulating army of crickets, following their own rules, sometimes turning right or left, always in a group. As they advanced they left behind a field stripped to the ground. They were following the fence line in a path forty-five feet wide and at least a mile long, crossing over the road, so in getting to the house, the truck ran over them, crushing their bodies, causing an explosion of crickets.

After Alex took pictures, which Fred planned to send to the media, we arranged to join Fred and his family later on. Then Buck and I headed over the Danforth Hills accompanied by a zillion advance-guard Mormon cricket scouts, jumping about our legs.

On June 18 we left Elk Springs and moved the camper several miles east of Craig. A few days later Buck and I saw Ruth come tearing down the road. She had driven 68 miles to bring us another one of her incredible lemon meringue pies. And to say still another last good-bye.

Three months later, when we were in Kansas, Buck received one of his many fan-mail letters. When I opened it for him, a crisp one-dollar bill fell out: ". . . and buy a chocolate bar for Buck. Love, Ruth."

While walking between Elk Springs and Craig, Colorado, a distance of 55 miles, I was admiring the rolling mountain plateau. The brush-dotted landscape sloped to the foothills of the Elkhead Mountains, which, in June, still wore a mantle of shimmering ice. A group of antelope sprang in unified leaps across the brush, stopping for a moment to watch us. "No, Buck." I soothed him, lightly tapping his collar. I knew what he had in mind. It would be fun to stir them up and have a chase across the hills. But I also knew that any rancher within shooting distance wouldn't waste a moment in bringing Buck down for having a fling at those graceful animals. "So don't even think about it, Buck." He thought about it, I could tell by the light in his eyes, but 1,500 miles on the road had taught him some useful manners.

For months I had been wondering what it would be like to climb the Rocky Mountains, a formidable 3,000-mile-long mountain range at least 300 miles wide. As beautiful as they are, the Sierras were no contest when compared with this massive mountain wall with over fifty skyscraping colossal peaks exceeding fourteen thousand feet within Colorado alone. When I lived in Denver, I had occasion to fly over them in a single-engine plane, and the raw cliffs and deeply gouged gorges had looked forbidding, an inhospitable land. If it was no place to set an airplane down, what could it be to walk it? Well, I'd find out, for we were at the Rockies' doorstep.

I stopped for a moment on the road to contemplate a 30-mile detour through a town named Streeter shown by a dot on my map. That was my mother's maiden name. But when I asked the occasional local residents I met, "What's out there?" they replied, "Nothing. Absolutely nothing." So I didn't go because I didn't want to see nothing; my memories of my mother are much too dear.

It started as a pain in my side, so I eased my steps, but the pain didn't go away. Instead of walking straight down the hill, I took it by zigzagging, as I had done when I was back in training, but that didn't help. I tried smaller, mincing steps until I was barely at a crawl. But oh how it hurt whether I walked or stopped. I kept on moving, but soon the pain was so blinding that I could barely breathe or think of where I was.

Alex found me standing on the side of the road unable to move. He helped me into the car by lifting my feet and setting them in after me. But what did we need to do? For a long while we had been careful about knowing where medical help could be found, but since Alex was in great shape now, we had relaxed somewhat on that score. The camper was on the top of Cross Mountain 15 miles behind me and Craig was 30 miles ahead. I was in pain so excruciating that Alex didn't bother me with questions. He turned the car, headed for the camper, and helped me, barely able to walk, into bed. My stomach was swollen, the skin stretched taut, and the pains came at regular intervals, almost as though I were in labor. Alex wiped my brow while thinking of what to do and brought me aspirin and a shot of brandy. He was trying to decide whether to move me again and drive at breakneck speed into Craig. But after what seemed an interminable time, the pains began to subside and I started to relax. Eventually I dropped off exhausted into a deep and long sleep.

I awoke to a sunny morning, raised my head, and looked out just in time to see a group of antelope bounding over a meadow. The ordeal was over—and no more special than cutting teeth. It was as though Nature called out one last time, making a final though painful statement, a monthly ritual natural to every woman, and another passage in a life was complete. What had begun three years before and could have been one more reason not to start out at all, instead merely marked the completion of a midlife transition. The periodical "kid stuff" was behind me. I entered, like countless women before and untold more to come, still another period of greater freedom, and if I had any regrets, well, there was a world of children out there and, in fact, I already thought of them as mine.

The day we walked into Craig, Olympic fever energized the air. Craig had been chosen as a night stop for the Olympic runner and he was due in town the next day. The chairman in charge of Olympic affairs was beside himself; there was still so much to do. Everything for the success of the festivities rested on his shoulders, so what do you do with a lady and a dog who just walked into town? Why, put her in the parade, of course.

So on June 25 we were there to celebrate with the exhilarated town the overwhelming, glorious, patriotic, and, perhaps, biggest day of Craig's history. Excitement was building, the runner was coming, and balloons still had to be filled. Had arrangements been made to have the jets fly overhead on schedule? People poured in from the surrounding counties and were jostling for position along the curb. Storefronts were decked out with banners and flags. The runner was ten miles away. Five miles now. Kids and dads and moms and grandparents—thousands lined the streets until, I was sure, there was no one left in the houses.

A few minutes before seven at the rosy end of the day, the murmur rose to a roar. There he is! The volley of the National Guards' twenty-one-gun salute shattered the air, and right on schedule, four jets made a flyover, screaming through the sky. All heads bent in the same direction. The impassioned all-American crowd cheered and waved their flags, and babies were hoisted to shoulders. The roar grew louder, people began chanting "U.S.A.," and as the runner passed by, the crowd began to follow him. Tears and laughter, mixed with sailing hats, filled the air.

Alex grabbed me. "Come on, we're next." I jumped into the car just starting to move, and a trail of police cars, fire engines, floats, trucks, and bicycles formed our parade and wound through the streets of town. In the midst of my excitement I caught a glimpse of Buck in the back seat. The charged-up energy of the crowd told him this was a special event and he sat up straight, turning his head from side to side as though the parade had been put on for him. We passed along Main Street and wound up a grassy hill to the Moffatt County High School. There a milling throng was waiting around the school parking lot, which was crowded with the fleet of thirty-seven Olympic vans. Cameras were rolling as the mayor officially welcomed the Olympic team. Then someone handed me the microphone.

What do you say to a crowd of ten thousand on such an inspiring day? Why, just what was in my heart: "How joyfully happy I am to celebrate with you the unique American spirit and to be here on this momentous day, which brought us all together." To my delight, the crowd roared its approval.

Still another extraordinary event had taken place only a few hours before. "Wouldn't it be wonderful to meet the Olympic runner along the way?" It was the last thing I'd said to Alex when Bucky and I headed out Highway 40 the same morning toward Hayden, 17 miles ahead. Had I known what Alex was thinking, though normally optimistic, I would have said, "Meet the Olympic runner? It simply can't be done." But Alex didn't know it could be difficult, and wonder of wonders, doors began to open for him, until he was given the name of an Olympic official to contact in Denver. After answering a multitude of questions from the Denver contact (which upon reflection appeared to have been a clearance), Alex was given a special code number and directions as to whom he should speak to in the Olympic vehicle.

It took two hours of anxious waiting, but Alex was finally given instructions and told of a certain location along the road, six miles east of Hayden, where a runner would arrive and the torch passed to a waiting relay. Everything was arranged, and Olympic officials at the Olympic run station were advised. The runner would stop, but not for long; the timing was precise.

Now nearly beside himself with excitement, Alex came tearing down the road and found us. With no seconds to spare he rushed me to the selected spot. The runner, splendidly bearing the Eternal Torch, was already in our view while the relay waited in position. And there, on an open country road, beside a weathered barn with the family from the farm looking on, the torch was passed to the relay, who then turned and handed it to me.

I was totally unprepared for this extraordinary, moving, improbable event, and tears welled up in my eyes. I tried to get rid of the lump in my throat, but "America, the Beautiful" is all I could manage to say, and the runner smiled—he knew just how I felt. I held the torch for as long as one glorious minute and then, mindful of the time, I handed it back to the next runner, who sprinted off. And can you believe it! Before they took off down the road, the Olympic caravan stopped to give me encouragement. Rolling down their van windows, hands waving, they gave the inspiring call "Go for it!"

In the first week of July I sat on the wooden steps of a little red schoolhouse with its pitched tin roof and small shingled bell tower. I was contemplating the road to my right. We were 15 miles east of Steamboat Springs, Colorado, and Buck and I had been on the road for only an hour. Already I was tired. "That's strange," I thought. "It isn't like me to start the day like this." I knew I had a ten-mile climb ahead of me, ten miles that would carry me to 9,243 feet at Rabbit Ears Pass, where I planned to continue another ten miles, following a high mountain plateau. I pulled a banana out of my pocket. It was part of my lunch but I was hoping it would give me a lift in energy now.

I was dawdling there in no hurry to shove off when a car pulled to a stop in front of where Buck and I were sitting, and a young lady smiled at me and said with astonishing ease, "Elena, I've been looking for you." She pronounced my name correctly, which is just a little off the usual, so I quickly searched my mind to find how we might know each other. As though she guessed what I was thinking, she said, "I heard you speak on the radio in Hayden and I drove out here to meet you. My name's Carol and I can't stay long." I invited her to sit on the steps with me and this is what she told me. "I used to be a stewardess but I've been living here in Steamboat Springs for five years now. Followed my boyfriend here. I have a really good job and I get to ski in the winter. It's really not all that bad. I'm not complaining. But," and she looked at me with eyes steady with composure, "something's been missing. When I heard you, I knew what it was. I've had a dream, but I was stuck in what I was doing, afraid to take the risk. What you said made me decide to do it." She paused a moment and then continued, "I want my life to mean something. I'm going into the Peace Corps. I wanted you to know that. My mother thinks I'm crazy, but I've already started to pack." She reached around my shoulders and gave me a long compassionate hug. "Gotta go—but I wanted you to know."

Another connection, another dream shared. All along the

way people had been reaching out, sharing dreams that had long been on hold, and every time someone did, I felt a surge of love emerge from the connection.

Well, the banana hadn't done it but Carol sure had. Buck and I started off down the road and began the ten-mile climb. The day was foggy, the grass at the side of the road was wet with dew. Up ahead, the yellow line in the middle of the road disappeared into a gray mist. But I wasn't cold. As a matter of fact, I felt hot. So I unzipped my sweat jacket at the throat, sat down on a large rock for a few minutes, and then pushed onto my feet and began again. We climbed some more miles and finally broke into the sun and now I could look over the tangle of brush at the side of the road, which was alive with delicate rose-colored blossoms, and down over a valley filled with a gauzy haze.

Buck and I took an early lunch. We left the road to climb down into a ravine through which a stream was trickling. I held my peanut-butter sandwich listlessly but it didn't go to waste. Buck swallowed it in one gulp before we pushed off again. The July sun was overhead so I removed my sweat jacket, but immediately felt cold, so I put it back on. Now more than ever before I concentrated on my breathing, no longer because of a morbid fear of height, but rather to try to get more oxygen into my lungs.

When I started my training for this journey, a friend had pointed out to me a fact about myself of which I'd been unaware: "You take such little breaths." She put her fingertips on her bosom and then flung her arms out wide. "You want to fill your lungs, give them the breath of life." I'd placed my fingers on my chest and thrown my palms outward, and almost collapsed coughing. "You do that while you walk and count one, two, three, four, while breathing in, hold two, three, four, then exhale, two, three, four, and repeat. You do that every day walking, you'll develop good lungs."

My lungs resisted. They were used to shallow breathing, so my gulps of air were uncomfortable and made my lungs tingle with an itch, then I'd cough. But I'd kept at it, one, two, three, four, and I began to stand up straighter. So when Buck and I hit the road, I remembered what I'd learned about breathing, and from the beginning I used a cadence, singing when I was alone, to the four-four beat of songs.

By midafternoon we had reached the plateau and I was relieved to not be climbing anymore. Buck picked up my mood and was unusually quiet. Then suddenly he broke loose and plunged down the side of the hill. I saw him as he caught up with a bushy-tailed marmot. He grabbed it by the skin on its back and shook it, brutally snapping its neck. He dropped the lifeless short-legged rodent on the ground and looked up at me, clearly puzzled, as though to say, this isn't the way it's supposed to turn out at all.

A dog will be what you want it to be. Bucky and I had been inseparable now for seven months, and he had adopted some of my nonaggressive traits. I had never seen him kill anything before and it made me sick. He nosed the marmot, trying to nudge some life back into it, but it didn't play anymore. Buck looked genuinely confused so I called him and he came running and we resumed walking, though neither of us with much animation.

At four o'clock I called it quits. I climbed up on the flat sun-warmed surface of a boulder in the middle of a mountain meadow, where I could watch beavers engineering their dam. That's where Alex found us.

That evening I barely touched my dinner, and went to bed early. "I just don't feel well" is what I told Alex. The next morning I woke up feeling as though I had been run over by a truck. My head was splitting and feverish and there was a dull rattling in my chest.

"It's just a cold," I told Alex. "All that walking out in the fresh air and sunshine, I can't possibly be getting sick. It'll pass in a day or two."

But two days later the rattle was heavy and labored and I had difficulty breathing. Alex was concerned. "I think you should see a doctor." I was still convinced it would pass in another day or two. However, Alex wasn't going to wait and see. He lifted my feverish hand and said, with just the right measure of insistence, "Elena, just to be sure, for my peace of mind, will you let me drive you to a doctor?"

For his sake I was willing. But what an effort for his peace of mind. Just getting dressed was more than I wanted to do.

The doctor took one look at me. "I'm afraid," he said with an air of professional concern, "that you have pneumonia. Let's just make sure." He took my blood pressure. "That can't be right," he said, and I wondered what that could mean. When he removed the cuff a second time, he looked at me and said, "But it is. Young lady, you have the blood pressure of a teenager." All that walking had resulted in something. Well, that was good news. However, the dark infected blotches on my lungs showed up on the X-rays.

There was absolutely no way I would be hospitalized. Compared with where I'd been, a hospital would be too confining, so alien to me I felt it would seriously slow my recovery. I wanted to be surrounded by trees and birds in the tranquillity of a mountain meadow. So I promised I would stay flat on my back and conscientiously take the heavy-duty antibiotics, and if that didn't do the trick, then I'd consider something else.

Alex compromised. He moved the camper closer to town. I was surrounded by trees and we were also closer to a telephone.

Now that I had given up resistance to being sick, I climbed under a blanket and let the illness take its course. My memory remains unclear about the next two days. I recall slipping in and out of sleep and not much more. Alex brought me water and my medication and wore a worried look he tried not to show. And poor Buck. He knew something was wrong and would not leave my side. When I'd awaken, his nose would be resting on the bed and he would be watching me with steady deep brown eyes. Alex had to take him outside from time to time, but just as soon as Buck was through he took up his vigil again.

Within two days the worst was over, though walking to the little bathroom was almost more than I could do. Now I had an insatiable thirst and was asking for juice and more juice, and in short order there was none left in the camper. Alex was reluctant to leave me for even a short while but I insisted. At my request he fastened the screen in place and left the door open wide to allow fresh air to enter. I was dozing when I heard men's voices just outside my window. Suddenly Buck was on his feet. A low powerful growl began to rumble in his chest and the hair on his neck and back stood up. Within seconds he threw himself through the screen, ripping it to shreds. When I got to the door, four big burly men stood riveted to the ground. The ferocity with which Buck kept them at bay was something to be seen. His lips were pulled back exposing a line of molars that I knew could crack a bone, and his one-inch canines flashed as he snarled horrible guttural growls.

The gentle dog who had slept by my side was now a ferocious beast. I saw the sweat on the brow of the man who was closest to the door and terror in the eyes of all. None of them dared to move. I knew that if they'd had any intent, other than curiosity, they wouldn't be thinking of it now. I called to Buck and he backed up to the camper, continuing to snarl his warnings. And the four unknown visitors jumped into a truck without looking back and hastily sped away.

By now Buck had met with thousands of people on our journey and there wasn't a thing he liked better than when people came out to join us on the road. I knew he was intelligent; he understood so easily what I wanted of him. But because he was so extraordinarily friendly, I had also sometimes wondered just what I could expect from him if the chips were really down. Now I knew. "You weren't taking chances, were you my friend?" I said as I patted him on the head. "Maybe we should have named you Gentle Hero instead." We continued to call him Bucky, of course, though sometimes we also now affectionately called him Gentle Hero, and he didn't seem to mind. He was ready to be courageous and the time would come when he would prove he'd truly earned that name.

Alex always seems to have a stockpile of what he calls "Grandma's Remedies," which he learned while growing up on his grandmother's farm, and now he was ready with another. He had discovered a mineral spring ten miles away. So for another week he insisted upon putting me into the car daily and driving to Hot Sulphur Springs. There, in a dank, dark, little cavelike room, he helped me sink into a pool of hot mineral water that spouted from a rocky cavern hole. He wasn't willing to take any chances on my not getting well.

On July 10 we were back on the road again. I was taking it slower but couldn't do that for long. We had almost two weeks of walking to make up. Bucky and I started where we'd left off, at the top of Rabbit Ears Pass. On a balmy summer day, in a beautiful alpine meadow, we wound our way back and forth across the Continental Divide. Try as I might, I couldn't make rabbit ears out of the rock formation that gave this pass its name. Nevertheless, the landscape was a mountain paradise: hills were braided with rivulets, and slender elegant conifers covered the mountains in what appeared from the distance to be a carpet of velvety green. Up there you might even consider that the Rockies are misnamed, as the meadow covering them is resplendent with a riot of wildflowers in random patches of radiant yellow, brilliant red, and the lavender-blue of the delicate columbine. And all these patches effectively overlay the massive upheaval of rocky crust below. Tranquil pools of limpid water sweep away to the east, with hardly a ripple on the surface, except for those made by beavers gliding through the water. That is, when they weren't standing on their dams chattering their teeth at us.

Buck and I had lunch with the beavers. I idly picked up a pebble and tossed it into the lake, watching the ripples spread, while fingering the penny in my pocket. That penny, which I was careful not to lose, had been given to me by a reporter back in California and I had been carrying it with me ever since. He had come to hear me speak at a school, and afterward had said, "Here, Elena," putting the penny into my hand, "take this for me, and please, throw it into the Atlantic if you get there, and make a wish for world peace."

Now I took it out of my pocket and looked at it. It was getting shiny from miles of fiddling with it. "Buck," I said to my friend sitting on the bank shoulder to shoulder with me, "if I threw this penny in the lake, it would make ripples as surely as the pebble did. And when the time comes when you and I throw it into the Atlantic Ocean, it will there, too, though we won't be able to see them in that pounding surf. But they'll be there and the energy from those ripples won't be lost. They'll even reach to other shores. You know, Buck, once you get there, there's no turning your back on the world.

"C'mon." I stood up and slapped him on the rump. "Let's move it—we've got a mountain to climb."

From the meadow we descended to the high-country mining town of Kremmling at 7,322 feet. There I found a diminutive version of Lady Liberty, barely taller than I, standing on a pedestal in the town square, as though to remind me of my final destination, still twelve months away.

We covered the 47 miles to Winter Park, one of Colorado's most popular ski resorts, and then began the eight-mile uphill hairpin climb to Berthoud Pass. By noon, Buck and I were on the last six miles of that dizzyingly steep, tightly convoluted road. The trees at the side of the road kept dropping away behind us, while in their shadows seedling conifers crowded for space and great patches of snow melted and seeped into the ground. I stopped to rest while looking over the limitless snowcapped evergreen mountains. Mt. Elbert, at 14,433 feet the highest peak in the Rockies, was nearby and the altitude of Berthoud wasn't far below it. We had made our way from 82 feet below sea level at Death Valley to nearly the top of Berthoud Pass. Could it possibly be, I thought with wonder, that it was only seven months ago that I was still working out on Old 20?

I didn't stay long. The glacial wind rustled the trees. I beat my fists together to try to warm my fingers, but my chest was tight so I concentrated on my breathing and pushed off. I knew that once I'd climbed this mountain I could never be the same.

When I started out across America, I'd looked at this journey as another path on which to carry on my own expansion, though I'd had no way of knowing then what it was that I'd learn. No university course could have prepared me, and up until the day I'd left I was thinking that at the end of the road I'd be returning home. Now everything I owned was in storage, and what, if anything, had I missed? My piano a few times, yes, but the places into which I was invited frequently had one, so I rarely felt at a loss. And where once I had taken pride in my being a fifth-generation Californian, I was finding that I was growing inordinately more proud of being a two-millionth-generation human, and that home would turn out to be every place. What was continuing to be of heartwarming value were the connections I was making with people. I was reaching out to America and America was reaching back, and my belief in the basic goodness of people was strengthening by the day.

Early in the morning Alex had moved the camper to the eastern downhill side of the mountain, ready to be moved in case something happened; my recovery from pneumonia was not far behind, so he was still wondering if I'd make it.

One hour later, in a late afternoon flurry of snow, we finally reached the 11,307-foot summit, where Alex, pride glimmering in his eyes, was waiting along with an Indiana family of four. The children endearingly held the congratulatory bouquet of carnations and mums that Alex had tenderly thought to buy. And then I looked off into the east, over miles of midcontinental plains. Out there lay my next challenge, the heartland of America, and my heart burst with the beauty of the land. It was now seven months into our journey. Buck and I had conquered the scathing heat of Death Valley and the seemingly endless enormity of the Rocky Mountains and everything in between. There simply could not be many more surprises ahead, I thought, but we would find out that there were.

NINE

•• •. .•• •• •. . .••.. .•• •. .• • • •. . . .•••.. .•• •. .•

Walking the Streets

It took ten days to come down the eastern slopes of the Rockies, down through the foothills, into Denver, a sprawling city and the scene of many good memories for me. We had dinner with tall, lanky Steve, one of my top-ranking former students, now a successful businessman; his wife, Joanne; and his fun-loving dad and good-hearted mom. From Denver we could have followed a track through the midsection of the country, but we decided to turn south instead to avoid the bitter Midwest winters. Our Southern detour added almost 400 miles to the journey, but we felt that the warmer climate in the South would more than compensate for the additional mileage.

We still had 255 Colorado miles to walk before we would reach the Kansas border, but after all the walking we had done, mileage had just become mileage. I remembered that back near the Utah border I had come to a highway sign that read, "Denver 414 miles." "Is that all?" I thought, and then had laughed at my reaction.

Alex was ready with more of his figures. "Elena, you know that the car gets about 27 miles to the dollar" (Alex has unusual ways of calculating things sometimes) "and that the R.V. gets a marginal, if we're lucky, six miles per dollar. Bucky has gone through thirty-six bags of dog food, so at that rate I figure he gets 70 miles to the dollar." But he had yet to compute how many steps I was getting to the dollar.

Fifty miles south of Denver we located the camper just outside of Colorado Springs. It was there that Buck had an experience that, in addition to the physical scars he now wore, would leave mental scars, some he has never forgotten.

On that August morning Alex and I were going over my itinerary for the day. The maps were spread over a table in a diner while Buck, as usual, was waiting in the car. The car had become his favorite place to be when he wasn't on the road with me. He felt safe and secure there and he could watch activity on the street. Frequently people stopped and said friendly things to him, which always made him grin with happiness. The car in a sense had become Buck's doghouse. Since it was summer, we were always very careful to leave him with a bowl of water, and sometimes we'd drive many additional blocks to be certain he was left in the shade. We always rolled the windows down far enough to give him currents of air, but not enough for him to crawl through and follow us into an eating place. This was a trick he would pull at every opportunity because he knew he stood a pretty good chance of catching the eye of a friendly waitress and getting a handout.

We came out of the diner ready to go and were stunned by what we saw. Buck was surrounded by six excited youngsters. Each had a stick, which they had shoved through an opening in a window. They poked at Buck while laughing and giggling and Buck was in a frenzy, crazed by the sticks jabbing his ribs, punching his rump, and poking into his neck. Whenever he yelped in pain, the children jumped up and down, laughed louder and shrieked shrilly in nervous excitement. Buck was in a rage. He snapped at the sticks, then whipped around and grabbed another in teeth now bared in a snarl. Buck was doing his best to defend himself, but he fought against unfair odds. Most unbelievably of all, while this outrageous offense was going on, two parents stood off to the side and watched.

Alex acted spontaneously. He ran to the car and jerked open the door. "Buck, get out," he commanded in a voice that would rattle the dead.

The children scattered. They threw their sticks in the air and ran to a nearby van, pushing each other while looking back over their shoulders. Then they jumped in, slamming and locking the doors. The parents froze in their tracks but recovered enough to fly to the van and leap in after the children. None of the family looked in our direction as they backed up and drove away.

Our hearts went out to Buck for having endured that painful, perplexing ordeal, and I saw by the flush in Alex's face how angry he was. My thoughts also went to the children, sorry for them that they had parents who allowed them to be so cruel. We refilled Buck's water bowl, which had been overturned in the fracas, and calmed him by patting him with our hands dipped in water until he stopped panting and trembling. However, to this day Buck will no longer allow himself to be encircled. He still loves children as much as ever. He shows it by running to greet them every chance he gets. He's met so many who have treated him well. But if he starts to feel crowded, he backs off, creating a safer distance, and I see the memory in his eyes.

It was the end of August. Now that we were out of the mountains and heading south on the plains, the weather really began to heat up. Tumbleweeds dried, broke loose from their roots, and cartwheeled across the road, sometimes bouncing against us before rolling over the barbed-wire fencing and tumbling across the plains. Buffalo burs dried into prickly-spiked balls. Then every few feet or so Buck would come to me and lift his paws, holding them up for me to clean out the nettles from between his toes.

Seventy miles from the Colorado-Kansas border, I visited the Las Animas School. From that day on, the young people of Ms. De Maio's sixth-grade class reached out and touched us by following our journey across the land, all the way to New York. Every time an envelope stuffed with all their letters tracked us down, their cheerful cross-country messages did more to maintain our spirits than they may have realized.

Those warnings that I had been receiving from well-wishers as I walked across the country, cautioning me to be careful of "all the bad things happening out there," were coming with less frequency now. I suppose it was, at least in part, because we had in fact already covered nearly half of the continent. And as a result of that, more than likely I was projecting an increased confidence and optimism. It would be at the end of September, somewhere between Garden City and Dodge City, Kansas, that Buck and I would reach our transcontinental halfway point. From that location we would have 1,950 miles to go.

Sometimes I stopped in at a truck stop for a plastic cup of orange juice to carry back on the road, and of course I would remember to bring a couple of oatmeal cookies for Bucky. In one of those places a red-headed waitress came to the counter to wait on me. "Hey, ain't you that lady I seen in the paper?"

"Might be," I answered, and she threw her palms in the air.

"Don't know how you do it," she exclaimed. But when I watched her running around in white sneakers at a hectic pace, bringing catsup, refilling endless coffee cups, and throwing playful banter back to the truckers, I figured that lively Emma, who must have been close to seventy if she was a day, was doing daily mileage that darn near came close to mine.

In the second week of September we entered Kansas, where

the prairie land is more than anything else a land of train whistles, silos on the horizon, and limitless, weedless rippling rows of wheat, corn, and milo (a kind of sorghum). The Kansas state song is "Home on the Range," but I saw no sign of the deer or the antelope, nor of the buffalo that had once roamed by the millions out on this plain. Looking over miles of repetitiously even rows of grain, I tried to imagine what early explorers had seen when they reported riding for days through herds of buffalo so dense they'd bring a train to a stop.

I still had fantasies about picket fences and apple-pie down-home goodness I was sure I'd find in Kansas, and indeed the people are as I'd expected. But farm wives now buy their eggs in the supermarket, chickens no longer peck for worms in the barnyard, and the farmer no longer has his fingers in the soil; the teeth of the reaper work at the land instead. The breadbasket of the nation has been mechanized on a grand scale.

We walked through miles upon miles of sunflowers facing east with us in the morning but turning their backs in the afternoon. The broad-faced flowers swivel their heads to keep their eyes on the sun. If there were ever any trees out on those plains, they'd given way to crops, so that on those days when the temperatures shot through the sky, we found no shade in which to seek shelter. Summer was still very much upon us, and shade we would have paid a ransom for was now as scarce as the hens. In Kansas we really sweated it out.

It was a rare day now when I wore a sweatshirt. I wasn't even carrying one tied around my waist. I kept my sweatpants rolled up to the knees and wore a cotton polo shirt. Buck continued to wear only his collar and surveyor's-tape ribbons and sank into irrigation water every chance he got. The pads on his feet were now thick enough to take on any kind of road, but there was no longer any hope for his rump; it was permanently faded.

I took a detour up a road where I could see farmhouses of the kind I'd expected to find. The crop in the fields had been harvested. It lay scattered where the reaper had moved across the field, gathered the crop, then compressed it into wire-baled bundles before dropping it onto the ground. But the house was empty, the family gone. Big industry owned the land. I had been told by farmers in the area that, one by one, family farms are sold off to "big business," which can turn a profit on the land, whereas the small farmer cannot compete successfully against industrialized farming methods. Five miles down that road we came to a deadend where I saw before me another empty home. The barn door was standing open, the small-farm equipment abandoned in the yard, rusting and wearing away. There wasn't a sign of the owners; it seemed they had walked away. The listlessly turning wind-mill made a doleful wailing moan as the sound vibrated down an empty well.

We arrived in Lakin, a small Kansas town 51 miles east of the Colorado border, and went to a convenience store. I pulled out all my coins, found two quarters, pushed them into the slot of a soft-drink machine, and gulped down a cola nonstop. I reached down into an ice machine and grabbed two fistfuls of ice cubes and threw them onto a sliver of shade against the northern wall. While Buck made short work of the ice I pressed my cheeks and palms against the cool of the bricks, then turned and rested my back against them, trying to get relief.

To prolong the comfort at hand, I walked down the main street and stepped inside the newspaper office. A lady in a polka-dot dress sat behind a desk, a fan whining over her head. She looked up. I had no reason to be there, so I simply said, "Whew, it sure is cool in here," to which she replied in a very sweet voice, "Only when you come in from the outside, dearie."

A man came out from the darkened back room. "Your dog looks thirsty," he said.

"He is."

He returned to the back room, where I saw him dump trash

from a wastepaper basket onto the floor and then heard the sound of running water. In another minute he was back with a basket full of water! Buck slurped noisily, sloshing all over the floor. I would have liked to stay for hours in that dim, cool room, talking with those friendly people, but we had mileage yet to make, so we said good-bye and stepped back outside into the glare of the sun.

Buck and I left Kansas on October 1 and entered Oklahoma. We spent days walking through land as desolate and arid as any desert could be. The monotony of the dry, treeless patch of land was just barely relieved by an occasional wisp of a cloud that quickly disappeared. It was the first week of October and still there were no signs of winter. Buck, in a relentless search for water, was looking in culverts in vain, sometimes lingering in the shade of those drains longer than was his habit. But he found not a drop of water and succeeded only in stirring up small, bony-plated armadillos. When Buck barked at the armored creatures, they simply rolled up into their shells and refused to listen to his commands.

Other than that, the only sound of activity out in that cheerless land was the heavy metal clunking of oil pumps unceasingly working. "Can't be much longer, Buck, before we come to water." He knew that word and may even have taken it for a signal, because he was off and running before I'd barely finished my sentence. It took me a minute too long to realize what he'd found. He'd already taken the plunge. Buck had seen the shiny surface of a pool of oil and thought it to be a badly needed puddle of water. I saw him just as he lunged and immersed himself, and then to my horror I saw him lap it up. It didn't take Buck long to realize he'd made a terrible mistake. When he stood up, black oil dripped from his flanks, and in no way could he fling it off.

But Buck was in luck, after all. We didn't have far to walk before we came to an old gas pump set back at the side of the road, and the young man, sitting in the shade of a lean-to, didn't have to ask what had happened. Without a word he brought gasoline from the pump in a can and some old rags, which we used to rinse the oil from Buck's hair. He even helped me scrub Buck down, after which we turned the hose on him to wash the gasoline off. And do you think Buck showed appreciation for our efforts? Not one measly bit.

Buck and I walked into Oklahoma City on the twenty-first day of October, but our arrival did nothing to lift my spirits. My normally optimistic mood was clouded by an undefined melancholy. Maybe it was just being in a city again instead of out on the land. Or simply the change of season I could feel in the air. Whatever it was, I found it hard to shake.

The streets we had chosen from the map would take me into the heart of the city, with a swing around the capitol and then north back out of town. We walked along streets that were old and worn, past houses in poor repair. An aged woman sitting on her porch smiled as we passed her by and I would have stopped to say a few words, but I spotted the kitten asleep in her lap and decided not to tempt Buck and upset the old woman's repose. Instead, I waved and continued on. We walked past darkened, gloomy houses, with torn curtains at the windows, and passed by a crumbling brick garage, when suddenly a truck pulled up to a stop and a man called out from the window, "Hey, lady, you shouldn't be walking here." His tone was rough, yet showed concern.

"Why?" I asked.

"Just take my word for it—it's best you don't."

"But," I persisted, "could you tell me why?"

"Lady, I'm doing you a favor. Take it at that." But he saw I was not easily frightened. He looked down at Buck and then back at me. "Well, with that there dog"—he hesitated—"you could be all right." And as quickly as he had appeared he sped away.

Well, that was a mystery. But I had no other way to get out of there than to walk it, so we continued on to the capitol and then turned north past dismal old motels. Buck and I were cutting through a vacant lot when I saw a slip of a girl in her late teens walking barefoot through the grass. She smiled when she saw Buck. "I got one of those," she said. "Hello, baby," she sweet-talked to him.

"Yours friendly, too?"

"Naw, mine—he's mean. My daddy, he got him for me. That where you got yours?"

"Not really." I answered noncommittally, though laughing to myself.

But the warning from the man in the truck continued to puzzle me, so the next day, over a cup of coffee, I asked about it. The waitress looked startled. "You walked there? Them's drug dealers and ex-cons in there. The other, that's prostitute row."

I was really low in spirit and I carried my gloomy mood out on the road with me the 90 miles to Tulsa and into the financial district. There I saw an enormous jack-o'-lantern looking down on me. It was perched on the roof of a modern mirrored skyscraper. A wave of sadness washed over me as I thought about the pumpkins in the fields back home, ripening on the vine.

I stopped to look in shop windows at fall coats and dresses, and then down at my baggy gray sweatpants. I was tired of wearing jogging shoes and sacky clothes. I saw an emerald green wool coat with a black velvet collar cut in classic lines on a sloe-eyed mannequin in a dramatic stance—and I wanted it. I wanted the bright color, the style, the newness, and I longed for a dress to go with it. I remembered that just a week ago I had stopped at a discount house to buy the fifth pair of eyeglasses to replace a pair lost in the woods. I'd looked over clothes hanging on the racks and believe it, there wasn't anything in that discount house that had not looked wonderful to me.

An unexpected late afternoon rain began to fall on my sweat-jacketed shoulders. I fought hard to keep back the tears but my vision blurred and my nostalgia deepened into a pit in the middle of my stomach as though I'd swallowed a cloud. So I turned away and walked down the dusk-lighted street and then on out of town.

But that night I called the kids back home. Just hearing their voices again helped to lift my homesick spirits. Everyone was well, but it was a reminder of what we were missing when I heard that little Kimberly, who was not yet five months old when we'd left, was already walking and Brandon was attending kindergarten. He had received the last of the postcards that I sent continuously so that he could follow our travels, and he had taken it off to school with him to share at show-and-tell. There, holding it up for his teacher and classmates to see, he had told them proudly, "This is from my grandma. She's out walking the streets."

TEN

·····•····•••••·····••··•••·····•••••·•·

Two Letters

We were still in Oklahoma, although not far from the Arkansas border, and my thoughts were running ahead. I had never been to Arkansas, so I was wondering what I'd find there. It was late October and the woods through which we were walking were quiet and very still when suddenly a tall, lanky man, with loose, sloping shoulders, stepped out from between the trees. He stood his ground in front of us, a rope between his hands, and his sudden appearance took me so by surprise that I stopped and returned his stare.

"That's a mighty fine-lookin' dog you have there, lady," he said in a wheedling drawl.

The blood chilled in my bones and I instinctively knew the answer when I asked, while looking him straight in the eye, "Is my dog in danger?" He looked back at me with eyes that would not hold my gaze. But I'd asked the question with straightforward simplicity; I was ready for the truth, and because I habitually see no enemy, the question held no rancor. Therefore, it had the surprising effect of clearing the air. He looked like a man who had expected a fight and was caught off guard when he didn't find one.

He shuffled the ground with the toe of his boot while cagily eyeing Buck before finally resigning himself to answer, "Naw, I guess not. Hey, he'd bite anyhow, wouldn't he?"

I lied about Buck when I answered, "Yes, he certainly would!" But I had read very recently in a local paper that the practice of putting dogs in pits where they fight to their death was widespread in the area. The thought that Buck might be kidnaped for that bloodthirsty sport had never crossed my mind before this very instant. Still, I intuitively knew without a shred of doubt it was what that man had intended, and one look at Buck told me why. All those miles climbing mountains and hours each day spent running around in the open had put Buck in prime physical condition. His eyes were bright, his muscles rippled, and his coat was a healthy sheen. Anyone looking to turn Buck into a savage pit-fighting beast would spot a winner in him. The idea of warping his gentle spirit and of his having to fight for his life in a bloody pit was too horrible to contemplate.

"You would have fought him," I said. It was a statement without accusation, so there was no need for a defense. "I've read about it." The man made no effort to walk away and I felt in no personal danger from him, so I said, "The dog and I have been walking awhile. I'm going to rest on that log. You want to join us?"

I had a motive in mind. I wanted to learn from this man how to prevent Buck from being abducted. And after fidgeting around a bit he allowed himself to sit.

"We're traveling through," I began. "Do I have to be careful for him?"

"Might be," he said, rubbing the knuckles on his hands. "Keep him out of the woods." Now he was as willing to be helpful as before he meant us harm. Perhaps he simply had a need to be heard.

"I don't want to lose him."

"Then keep him close and keep moving."

"I thought it was illegal."

"It is."

"Then why doesn't the law step in?"

"What if the law do come by? Give 'em a beer, let 'em place a bet. They look the other way. Don't take long to dig a pit, you know. Someone comes by, acting suspicious-like? Just throw plywood over the hole. Or cover it up with a truck."

"How do people know?"

"Word of mouth."

"And then?"

"Put 'em in a pit. He don't stand a chance, though. He'd be torn to shreds."

"And the men?"

"Rootin' fer the one they got money on."

"They do that with a dog that has become a friend?"

"Don't keep 'em long enough for that."

"I heard it's done with roosters, too."

"Yeah. Only don't let them kill each other; them's too valuable."

Well, I didn't learn much about protecting Buck except "Keep him close and keep moving" and so that's what we did. We had gone maybe another 20 miles and were heading for the Arkansas River when I glanced across the road and up an embankment. Sitting up there not far from the edge, along the fringe of the woods, was a house trailer resting on concrete blocks, with a scavenger's collection of junk scattered around the yard. In the shadows beneath that dwelling I could see two sets of eyes stealthily watching me.

Without warning, two stocky pit bull dogs struggled out from underneath that trailer. To my horror I saw that neither one was chained. My blood ran cold. Without hesitation, they charged down the steep embankment and rushed toward me. They were the ugliest, meanest-looking dogs I'd ever seen. Neither was as tall as Buck, but they had squat, thick bodies, built low to the ground, with jaws that narrowed and jutted out. One of those creatures had a black mark like a patch across one eye. There was no mistaking their terrifying power or where their aggression was directed. I was the target. I froze to the ground; there was no time to think of a defense. "Buck!" I screamed, knowing he lagged behind, as they leaped like a pair in step. At that moment I felt a rush of air as Buck flashed by and with a death-defying howl leaped onto the backs of the two, rolling them both on the ground.

What followed next was so violently grisly I want never to witness it again. The dogs fought in a vicious tangle, each one trying for advantage. Buck would have one at his throat while the other had a grip on his thigh, mauling and tearing his flesh. Buck fought back with savage intent, although he didn't have the odds. Blood spurted from wounds slashed open, and there was so much of it smeared on their fur that it was hard to tell from which dog it came, but I saw skin hanging loose from Buck's eye. One dog hung cruelly on his jowl, the other had a grip on his leg.

I looked around on the ground for a stone to bash at the dogs and found instead a stout length of a limb that had fallen from a tree. I flung away my walking stick and grabbed hold of the sturdy branch. Then, using it as a battering ram, I came up behind Buck and rained blows upon the pit bulls. I smashed and bludgeoned and aimed for the nose and jabbed in the most painful spots. In this way together, Buck and I routed them off. We drove those murderous skulking brutes back across the road, though they stopped to look back menacingly once more before they continued on their way.

I wiped Buck's wounds the best I could, with the clean inside of my jacket, and smoothed on the antiseptic bag-balm salve, which I now carried with me at all times, though never would I have suspected that it would be used for this purpose. Buck did his part by licking the blood from the scratches in my palms. It would seem darn near impossible, but nevertheless it was true, that the bond between us grew instantaneously deeper and stronger than it ever had been.

Later, Carl, a talk-show host, tried his best to make me reveal any bias I might have about the South. "This is the South, lady," he growled. "Doing something like what you're doing? Don't expect my listeners to be easy on you. You're a Yan-kee lady." He dragged it out to make his point. "Expect it will get rough." But after we had spent an hour on the air, with Carl doing his best to stir up the dust, he turned to me and said, "Stay on for a second hour. It'll help me hold on to my Donahue listeners!"

But the most difficult (if you can call it that) questions I got were from a man who demanded to know, "Are you a secular humanist?" It was clear by the tone of his voice that sure as heck I'd better not be. Tell you the truth, I wasn't exactly sure just what he meant or what he wanted to hear, but apparently I answered properly. "Are you a feminist?" he added. I knew what that mean, all right, and he was undoubtedly surprised at my answer.

"Oh, yes! Most positively I am," I'd said, "although I am as well a masculinist, even though that word is not in the dictionary. You see, if 'ist' at the end of a word means 'in support of,' well, I really don't know of any group of human beings I am unwilling to support."

But the real difficulty in walking that part of the South came from a lonely isolation of a different kind from what I'd known while walking out in the desert. It was autumn, and my homesickness, though greatly relieved by my phone call back home, continued to hang on.

My itinerary called for me to follow highways that paralleled Interstate 40 right to the heart of Arkansas. At Little Rock I'd pick up Highway 70, and if things turned out as planned, Buck and I would reach the border of Tennessee around December 10. The big cities came closer together now, but autumn had brought its blustery weather, so fewer people were out on the streets. The holidays were coming up fast, pulling on my emotions. It was a time when I had more thoughts of home than ever. Even though we had gone south for the winter, temperatures continued to drop. We began to pass by more homes with smoke curling from the chimneys. I saw families and fireplace warmth inside, while Buck and I were on the outside, looking in from the streets. So I accepted more invitations to talk in schools and places where people gather, and between those locations I hurried, trying to outdistance my homesick sentimentality.

We strode along with purposeful steps past murky bayous where trees, hung darkly with Spanish moss, stood on roots that stretched to reach out of the water, where croaking toads grew silent until we had passed them by. Carl's warnings came back to me when we hurried beside railroad tracks, grass growing between the ties, and where gaping boxcars stood empty except for the shadows inside. Pickup trucks flew by with rifles fastened across back windows, and white and black faces peered through rain-splattered windows trying to make sense of a woman and a dog walking along the road.

Near Carlisle, I saw four shirtless men in a field, their skin shiny with perspiration. Two of them worked the earth with shovels, preparing a pit in the ground. The others scraped the white-lard hide of an enormous slaughtered hog, preparing it for a barbecue. I waved but they turned away as though they were afraid of me. Closer to Brinkley, a woman ran down her driveway and, cupping her fingers around her mouth, yelled across a drainage ditch, "How many miles now? Saw you on TV." She warmed me by waiting where the driveway met the road and invited us into her house. While roofers pounded above, she served root beer to me. Buck lay on the kitchen linoleum, drinking the family dog's water and gobbling down his food.

Buck and I pushed hard, trying to walk off my nostalgia. We passed rice and milo and cotton fields, and one day I found Israel sitting in his big sedan, the molasses color of his car matching his skin. He murmured, while looking over the cotton with the saddest, deepest eyes, "Them fields—that's where I spent my life. Come back to look sometimes. Wife's dead. Kids gone. Forty years I picked cotton. Yes, sir, in them days—more'n five hundred pounds a day. Yes, ma'am, shore did."

A cold wind was blowing over the fields, rattling my dismal mood. I had forgotten my gloves that day so my fingers were red and stiff. Buck lightened the mood by chasing after a tuft of cotton that had blown loose from a drying twig, and again fell into the water, thinking, I suppose, that what looked to be cyprus needles floating on the bayou were strong enough to support his weight.

Then for the first time I noticed that ice was forming on the rim of standing water, so I ran to keep Buck warm, and I fought to keep back the tears.

But then I received two letters I had been hoping for. They came from two boys I had met in a most unsought-after way. Receiving their letters in the midst of my mood made all the difference.

I'd met the boys a number of weeks before and I was beginning to think maybe they wouldn't write. On the day we met I'd been walking on a stretch of road where for a while I had watched a yellow harvester droning monotonously on the horizon and then closer still, a locust struggling under a clump of withered grass. It was late in what had seemed to be a never-ending summer, when the temperature dropped 40 degrees overnight. Months of sweaty days and sleepless nights were over. I could smell it—autumn was on its way.

While walking along the road, I was enjoying the drowsy warmth of the sun on my skin, noticing that already a faint wind whispered warnings of a not so distant winter. But of course we were going south to avoid the colder half of the year, so we had no need to worry.

Then abruptly I was hit with a raw and piercing pain. I doubled over and spun around grabbing at the burning sensation expanding in my groin. "A snake—a snake" I yelled. It came to mind because we'd often seen them on the shoulder of the road, where they slithered to bask in the warmth left there by the sun. I swiftly searched the ground knowing full well that I'd better know which kind of snake had put its fangs in me in order to be treated.

But I didn't find a snake. I found instead two young boys playing with a gun, which I later learned was not a toy but potentially a deadly weapon. They had seen me coming, raised the gun, and pulled the trigger. They were in a yard where weeds tangled with shrubs and the lawn had been neglected for so long it no longer needed cutting. From the road I could easily see the boys in the grass but neither would look at me.

The older boy couldn't have been much older than eleven. He was letting marbles drop one by one from his fingers onto the grass, while the younger, by a couple of years, was lying on his stomach, his ankles locked in the air, and both were trying their darnedest to avoid looking at me. The gun was shoved under the younger boy's chest, partially hiding it from view. While this may be difficult for a few to understand, nevertheless it is true: my heart went out to them. Later I talked with a man who told me, "I would have beat the ———— out of them." But they already evidenced telltale signs that led me to believe that they'd already been handled in that counterproductive way.

I could tell by the way they were pretending to be cool that they were hoping I wouldn't press it. Years of working with youngsters, many of whom had been angry, left no doubt in my mind that they weren't angry at *me*—how could they be?—but they did hold resentment against what had happened in their lives.

Frankly I was nervous about turning my back on them but was fortunate in that a sheriff's car was parked a short distance up the road. So, looking back from time to time, I made my way up there. Buck had returned from running in a field and now trotted along beside, sniffing in the air. He seemed to know that something was wrong, though he couldn't know just what.

"I've been shot," I said through the officer's open window. It was blunt, but what else could I say, and it certainly woke him up.

"You have, where? What happened? Just a minute," he said as he jumped out of the car. "Do you need attention?"

"No, at least not right away."

I saw him study me and reflect on that answer, but he saw no signs of panic, so he reached for a pad and pencil. "All right," he said, "let's start with your name."

"It isn't why I'm here."

"It's not?" He must have thought, What else could she want than to make a report of it?

"I was walking along the road up there when I was hit in the groin. I looked around and I saw two boys and they have a gun."

"Can you describe the kids?"

"Sure."

"I think I know who they are. One of them plays with my boy. Basically they are good kids."

"Why I'm here is that I'd like to go back there and talk with them. It's obviously dangerous what they did, and if we use your uniform in the way it's intended, we might just be able to say something that could make a difference to them, hopefully, for the rest of their lives."

"You want to do that?"

"Of course. Do you?"

The yard was empty and the boys were gone so we climbed the wooden stairs. On the top step, pushed against the siding, was a green and yellow box of pellets.

The sound of afternoon television came through an open window. After three sharp raps the door was opened just a little. Standing inside in his stockinged feet was the smaller of the two, looking very frightened when he recognized me.

"Is your mother home?" I asked.

He sized me up, swinging the door by the knobs while he

balanced on one foot, but he made no effort to call his mother.

"What's your name?" I asked in a voice intended to show him that I had not returned in anger.

"Rick." He barely whispered it while looking down to study the foot he was twisting on top of the other.

"How old are you, Rick?"

"Ten."

"The other boy. Is he your brother?"

He glanced at me swiftly.

"Is he your brother, Rick?"

He nodded.

"What's his name?"

"Chris."

"How old is Chris?"

"Almost twelve."

"We'd like to talk to your mom and your brother, Rick."

He looked at me for a moment; his tough look was trying to win. Then abruptly he pivoted on one foot and disappeared down a hallway, leaving the door standing open.

We waited, wondering what was happening, when a woman appeared at the door. She was nervously drying her hands on a towel. Anxiety tightened her brows. "Yes? Is there something you want?"

"Ma'am," Officer Craig began, "this lady was shot. About twenty minutes ago walking past this house. We'd like to talk to you about the boys. Are you their mother?"

She turned around to the boys, who were peering from behind her back. "Were you playing outside with the gun?" she demanded, but she knew the answer. "Were you out there with your gun?" she screamed. The boys squirmed. "I told you not to play with it!" Her hand flew to her head, grabbing her hair by the roots. "My boyfriend gave them that gun," she exclaimed as though that would explain. "I made them put it away. I didn't know they were out there with it."

Officer Craig and I spent considerable time with them. He

emphasized the dangers of playing with guns and I know it helped, but when we left I glanced over my shoulder to nod another good-bye, and caught the expression on Rick's face and heard his nervous giggle when he nudged his brother in the ribs and his lips formed "Told-ja." I knew then we hadn't gone far enough and that I wouldn't leave the area until I'd done what I could to help those boys along.

"We'll have to make a report on this," Officer Craig said, but I was already thinking about how I would proceed.

"I don't want them to have a record."

"We have to. In cases like this it's required."

Later that night I went back, and my knock was answered by their mother, whose face grew pale when she saw me. It could be quite natural for her to assume that I had come back to cause them trouble. But I hadn't. "Hello," I said in a way that I hoped would not sound threatening. I waited a moment before I went on—she looked so very frightened. How could I have her understand that regardless of what had happened I could love her boys as well as I had many, many others, and that if we handled this situation right, the boys and I could make something of it. "I did not come back to cause a problem for you, and if you don't mind, I'd like to speak to the boys."

"No," she said, and her eyes were clouded with fear. "They've already gone to bed." Then, as though this would really do it, "And they've already gone to sleep."

So I know I must have surprised her when I said, "Then, please wake them up, if you would, because what I have to say could be helpful, and would you be there, too?"

She hesitated but must have sensed that I meant no harm because she opened the door, stepped back, and led me to the living room, where I waited on the couch while she went to get the boys. As they came down the hall, they whispered so that I could not hear, then appeared in rumpled pajamas and sleepy, frightened faces. They got down on the carpet in front of me, wiggling around to get comfortable, while their mom sat on a nearby chair gripping her knees. "I came back because

I want to know you." I let that set a moment, then went on. "My dog, Bucky, and I have been walking across the country. We started on the Pacific Coast and so far we have come this far." I waited a moment to make certain they understood before I went on again. "Can you imagine why?"

They did not answer and their mistrust of my motives was evident. "We're doing it to see America, and it's turned out that the more I see, the more I love it." Again I waited before I told them, "And you are part of it."

"Today you shot me. We're lucky, the muscle will repair. But if you'd shot my eye, it would not. And if you'd shot my dog, you know, I might have lost my friend forever."

Just as I'd hoped, Buck got to them. I stayed several hours that evening telling them about Buck's adventures, how he was bitten by a rattlesnake and how his strength had pulled him through, how he had got lost and how joyful we were when reunited, and how faithfully he had watched over me when I was sick. I told them these and many more stories about Buck's bravery and loyalty until I was sure they knew him and felt their natural compassion for him. Their relaxed expressions told me that, at least for the moment, they had forgotten to be angry. The time was right to ask, "Do you know what I'd like you to do?"

"What?" By the way they asked, I knew we had crossed the line.

"I'd like you to write to Buck. All the way to New York."

"Would he answer?" Rick whispered timidly.

"I promise he would. He'd get help from me, but that would be okay, wouldn't it? You could ask things like, 'How many more mountains have you climbed, Buck?' or 'How are the pads on your feet?' and even 'Has anybody else shot at you?' "

There it was—out in the open. The boys' eyes darted at me but I wanted to bring the whole thing right up to the surface. I had no bad feeling about the boys and I wanted them to have none for me. We had to clear the air. No more hiding behind excuses like "I didn't do it" or "We didn't do it." Because once it was out on the table, the boys had no reason to hide, and they promised they would write.

When I stood up to say good-bye, they scrambled off the floor. I saw what they wanted to do, so I held my arms open to them and they rushed right in.

When I received their letters, you can imagine what it meant to me. I had reached out to them and they had reached back to me. The depression I had been carrying vanished with their letters. The boys had kept their promise.

They told me some things they had been doing, and Chris's letter ended, "and we see how far you've gone. We're proud of you. We want you to make it." Rick's letter started with "I am sorry I shut you" and closed with "You are the best persons I ever met." Those two boys will remain my friends as long as they want to be.

ELEVEN

....

Holidays on the Road

On the fifteenth day of December we entered Tennessee, where, in a little less than two months, we walked 575 rolling miles—the second greatest mileage covered in any one state, surpassed only by California's 600 miles.

From the middle of December until mid-February, we planned to handle the Tennessee route by having the gas-eating Home Sweet Home follow the shortest route. That would be along Interstate 40, while Buck and I would take the more circuitous and ever more interesting Highway 70. That would put us sometimes north and sometimes south of the interstate artery, and lead us through the cities and towns of Memphis, Nashville, Cookeville, Knoxville, and the communities in between. Finally we would reach Bristol, the town that straddles two states. That would occur during two winter months, encompass the entire holiday season, and include the second birthday I spent on the road.

I was now on my twelfth pair of shoes, as I changed them regularly for the benefit of maximum resiliency in the soles.

While I had anticipated that by this time my legs might have muscles to resemble those of a wrestler, that never seemed to happen.

On our first day in Memphis, Buck and I had come down Riverside Drive and were standing on the banks of the muddy Mississippi, watching animated passengers hurry up the red-carpet ramp to board a riverboat. Luggage and last-minute supplies were being toted aboard. Even so, amid all that excitement, Buck and I were invited to board and have a look around. The polished luxury in the cabins and dining rooms made me more aware than ever of how much our lives— mine, Alex's, and Buck's—had changed.

The *Mississippi Queen* seemed a strange place indeed for Buck—and I wasn't the only one to think so. Passengers would turn and stare as Buck, totally undisturbed by the unfamiliar surroundings, padded over the decks. But the manner of travel was so totally different from the way that Buck and I were traveling that I felt as alien as someone might who had descended from the moon. Accordingly, after getting a look at the boat, and especially its dramatic fire-engine-red paddle wheel, we hastened to get off.

But the visit to the riverboat started me thinking about Buck's adaptability. Of the three of us his flexibility struck me as being the most remarkable. He had made a successful adjustment from an idle, house-lounging dog to one who could enter into any situation and take it in stride. He had followed me as easily into the desert as he had through traffic-jammed cities. He had just strolled the decks of the *Mississippi Queen* and had shown as much dignity there as when he'd been invited to meet members of church congregations. And when you stop to think about it, he hadn't even been given a choice.

Certainly one of the most unusual situations he had yet been in was when we were back in Tulsa and the newspaper wanted a picture. We stopped off at the downtown office on our way through town, and after passing the building security guard who sort of raised his brows, we rode the elevator to the newsroom. It was in the stark white photo studio where I was most concerned about Buck. He was surrounded with lighting equipment that seemed to hang from everywhere, covering ceiling and walls. When the battery of lights flipped on and the brilliance zoomed in on him, I wondered immediately what I could expect from him. But I had no need to worry. He acted as though he'd been born to sit for photographs.

It hadn't always been so for Buck, nor, for that matter, any of us. Way back at the beginning of our trek, we'd all had to learn how to handle the unusual demands of the road.

The first weeks were particularly hard on Buck. We were only three weeks away from home, and still enduring that period when it seemed that everything that could possibly happen was happening to us. I noticed some lumps beneath his skin. On closer examination I discounted insect bites as the cause. I didn't rule out that he might have run through bushes to which he was allergic. As the days went by, the lumps multiplied at an alarming rate until there was no mistaking it: Buck was one heck of a lumpy dog.

We were passing a community that was so small I doubt it could have had a name. There were just a couple of stores on the road. One was an old-fashioned pharmacy. Apothecary jars stood in the window, and inside, along a wall, was a soda fountain. I left Bucky outside and went in for two vanilla ice-cream cones. One thing led to another and I got to talking with the pharmacist about Buck's lumps.

"Let's take a look," and he stepped outside with me. "Humm," he said while scratching down into the hair. "I'd say Buck has a real good case of hives. Give him a couple of Sleep-eze or Sominex—that should do the trick."

"Sleeping pills for Buck?" Buck had never had trouble sleeping. And now that he spent his days outdoors with me, you could bet that at night he would be the first asleep.

"It's the antihistamine; should reduce the swelling. Buck's

probably a little nervous. It will make him a little drowsy so that he can relax."

The idea sounded crazy but if it would help, why not? "How much should I give him?"

"Buck's big enough for an adult dosage."

That night I took two tablets and naively tossed them to Buck just as I might a cookie. Buck caught them and promptly spit them out. Then I thought I'd be clever and pressed them into cheese. It took him no time at all to separate the pills from the cheese and spit them out again. "All right, Buck, two can play that game." This time I got smart. I had him sit and then straddled him as though he were a horse. Meeting with some resistance, I pulled back firmly though carefully on his muzzle and separated his teeth. That way I managed to open his mouth. Then I dropped the pills down into that enormous cavern of a mouth, and because I was now on to his tricks, I held his jaws closed until I felt him swallow.

In no time at all Buck was sound asleep on his spine with his feet up over his head. As a matter of fact, he was so relaxed that his lips fell away from his teeth and he set up a howling snore. Buck was no Sleeping Beauty. All dignity to which I have previously referred was gone. But the antihistamine did the job. The hives disappeared, and once Buck got used to the road, they never reappeared.

We watched while the last bags were loaded aboard the *Mississippi Queen*. Then, getting our bearings again, we headed into town. The shop windows we passed were decked out in holiday spirit, reminding me that with every passing day we increased the distance between us and family and friends back home. It seemed quite impossible to me that it was only a year earlier and at another Christmas that I was training on Calistoga Road for this journey.

"Would you have gone if you had known in advance what was in store for you?" It was a question often asked. And after thinking the question over, I had to answer yes. It was ever so much clearer to me than it had ever been before that of all the pleasures there are in life, the most satisfying and most enduring come from reaching out to others and feeling others touch you back.

Buck and I were standing at the curb waiting for a break in the traffic. The haunting notes of a saxophone slipped from a second-story window and trailed down into the street. Suddenly a big and flashy car pulled up to the sidewalk, close enough to where we were standing to almost run over our feet. The plump shoulders of the woman sitting behind the wheel were draped in a dark fur stole, and when she leaned across the seat and pushed the passenger door open, the smell of her perfume rushed out. Her hair was stacked in a tangle and she wore large-stone, gaudy rings on every one of her fingers. Two more women, loaded down with parcels, rushed out of the shopping mall. One grasped the front of her full-length mink, closing it against the wind, and the other held on to her hat. They threw their parcels into the back, and the driver, in a rush, called out, "Hurry up—get in!" That's where Buck gave an outstanding demonstration of just how far he had come in following a command.

He cleared the shoulders of the women in the car without so much as touching a single hair. That ninety-three-pound Doberman sat in the back seat, grinning, proud of what he had done. The woman shrieked hysterically, scrambling with topmost speed to clamber back out of the car. They were laughing uncontrollably and so driven by their nerves that none could hear, nor would have believed, my hurried exclamations: "He's friendly—he's really friendly—believe me he really is!"

They stood gasping in a huddle, clutching one another that way, and were so frightened that I would not have been surprised at all to see them faint away. After a while they calmed down and I called Buck from the car. The driver, the one with the beehive hair, rummaged inside her purse and brought out a pocket of mesh stitched in the shape of a boot. It was tied with a red satin bow and stuffed with bone-shaped biscuits, really more fitting to a poodle than a dog of robust size. "It's Christmas, Buck," she said. "I bet we scared you, too." And though she tried, she just couldn't bring her fingers close to his mouth, and so she tossed the pocket of biscuits to him.

Occasional snow and sleet accompanied our 47-mile walk into Jackson, Tennessee, and when the wind howled along the road it made our passage ever so much worse. A bleak winter sky kept a dreary pall over the terrain so that when blackbirds swirled about overhead in flocks of enormous size, I welcomed them for their cheerful twittering chatter. At times they'd land all at once upon a field, and occasionally I would see someone come out of a house and stand in the yard banging pots and pans together, making a racket to send the birds back into the air. Other times they'd settle down on the road in front of us. But when we'd get too close for their comfort, they'd lift in a fluttering swirl, to settle again and pick the grain from another farmer's field.

Over the months Buck and I had developed a great tolerance for temperature variations. In summer we had adapted to extremes of heat and now we were adjusting to the cold. When I came in from walking, cheeks ruddy from the cold, the 70-degree temperature inside Home Sweet Home felt like a sauna to me. I would shut the heater off and Alex would turn it on. At one minute the temperature would be for me a comfortable 60 degrees, and a few minutes later I thought it felt more like an oven. Of course we compromised. After that, late in the evenings when we both were in the van, Alex might, while at the computer, look more as if he had prepared for a scaling expedition on Mt. Everest than for an evening at home, whereas I might be answering Buck's fan mail in a short-sleeved shirt. And Buck would find his comfort sleeping in the draft on the floor.

Alex had been given permission to put Home Sweet Home at the rear of the Jackson Holiday Inn. While a tarmac lot cannot compete with a riverbank location, the comfort and convenience of parking in the lot more than compensated for the view. Stopping there meant quite simply that we had electricity. We could use the computer and our little heater without belching volumes of smoke and noise from the generator. From that spot we looked down on the roof of the home of Casey Jones, the engineer of railroad fame, and listened to holiday music emanating from a nearby restaurant. It was piped into the lot without interruption every single night. We figured that in a very few days we had undoubtedly heard "Silver Bells" at least three hundred times.

During the final six months of our journey, Home Sweet Home was parked in the lot of numerous Holiday Inns. It was convenient for us especially during the winter months when finding a camp location was difficult, at best. Buck just loved those stops. Somehow he would manage to persuade softhearted personnel to save good meaty scraps from the kitchen. As a result, Buck may be the only dog in America who gets really excited when he see the Holiday Inn roadway signs.

We met Frances in Jackson and she really brightened our Christmas by inviting us to a dance. She and her friend picked us up and it's a darn good thing they did. Otherwise, never in a million years would we have found Finger, where the dance was held. We traveled way back deep into the woods, halfway to the Mississippi state border, by following a rambling road that twisted and turned and always seemed to swing back upon itself. What I seem to remember now is that we turned left at the "old burned tree" and I believe right at "Uncle Jed's," both of which you couldn't see because they were no longer there. We eventually came to a clearing where hundreds of cars were scattered under the trees surrounding the Finger High School gym. How anyone knew to come out there at all still remains a mystery to me.

But they came, all right. And even before we were out of the car, I could hear the finger-snappin', foot-stompin' banjo-and-fiddle twang of a real live country band. People had come down out of the hills and poured on out of the woods to dance, by golly, and that's what they meant to do. While the fiddle sawed a jee-jaw twang and the banjo plinked away, the nasal voice of the caller sang "Swing you partner" to the fast-steppin', quick-hoppin', stompin' beat of hillbilly "Cotton-Eyed Joe."

This was no slow hanging-on-to-each-other shuffle nor do-it-by-yourself gyrations, no-sirree. This was real country mountain music, and what I liked best was that there was no such thing as a wallflower among these folks. Two big hand-holding circles took care of that. Twist to the right, swing to the left, "Grab your partner in front of you . . ." And your partner could just as well be seven years old or seventy, or any age in between; the purpose was to whoop it up, have uncomplicated, good-ol'-fashion', one big heap of fun.

A rustic-looking gentleman, dressed up for the occasion in a red-checked shirt and brown string tie, his white hair parted on the right, walked up to me and, polite as he could be, asked me to dance the "John Paul Jones." He didn't wait for an answer. Before I knew what was happening he'd spun me onto the floor. Now, unless you're raised on the "John Paul Jones," it's much too complicated to step right in and dance. He probably took it for modesty when between whirlwind spins I tried to tell him that I really didn't know how to dance.

"That's all right, ma'am. I want me a chance a-dancin' with the walkin' lady. Just foller what I do." He had to believe me, all right, when I tripped him over my shoe. He stopped right there dead in his tracks in the middle of the floor and said, in his gentlemanly way, "Don't worry none 'bout what I'm doing. I'll just foller you."

By the time we got to Nashville we were no longer under any illusions! Going south meant freezing weather. Every day I wore my heaviest weather-resistant jacket with the thick furlike lining and piled many layers under it. It was a rare day when the hood of my sweatshirt was not in place before I stepped out the door, and then it was frequently covered with a knitted cap over which I pulled the jacket hood and pulled those strings up tight. I was never without my old leather ski mittens or thermals under my sweats. I wore two pairs of socks, one of which came up to the knees. I still wore the same kind of heavy jogging shoes I'd been wearing all the way. My feet were always on the move, stirring up heat inside the shoes, so even in the snow the sneakers worked out fine for me. Buck wore my red-hooded sweatshirt more often now, the sleeves rolled into a cuff just above his ankles. Sometimes he wore the green. Both made him highly noticeable against the snow so that when he was dressed like that a hunter was unlikely to mistake him for a deer.

On the night of December 31, about 20 miles from Nashville, we heard a light tap on the camper door. Standing outside in the snow was a lady I'd never seen. "Wanted to know if anything bad happened to you in Tennessee," she asked.

I was startled by the question. "No, not a thing," I told her, searching for a reason for her question.

"Just wanted to know. I'd want to do something about it. You know, take responsibility for it. Wouldn't want you to leave Tennessee with a bad impression of us." She held up a bowl. "Wanted you to have this. I knows yer a long way from home. It's hog jowls and black-eyed peas. It's what we have on New Year's."

TWELVE

•••,•••••••,•••••,••••••,••••••,••••••,•••

Closing in on the East

Buck met her in Nashville on the steps of the Parthenon (a replica, of course, but according to the plaque, "the only one in the world"). She was sitting between two columns, and when Buck caught sight of her, his eyes sharpened in a focus as they always did when fixed on something of interest. On that windy day Buck fell head over heels in love with a basset hound.

She was as different from Buck in stature as any dog could be. Where Buck is tall and slender, Farla was short and squat and her ears hung all the way down to her feet so that she nearly tripped on them. Her legs were bowed and short and so incredibly stubby they couldn't lift her belly, so it rested on the ground. Nevertheless, on that day it certainly looked to me that Buck had fallen in love, and she obviously thought he was grand as she tumbled down the stairs to greet him. They romped and played over the grass and up and down the stairs of Nashville's Parthenon. He was careful not to step on her but perhaps the surest sign of his affection was that he let her nibble the surveyor's ribbons still tied around his neck. Of all the dogs he met she was the only one given that concession.

Of course we couldn't stay as long as they would have liked. When it was time for us to take to the road, Farla howled and yelped in distress and made a pitiful fuss when swept into her owner's arms and carried away. As for Buck, it seemed his heart would break. He tugged and pulled, whimpered and whined, as we started out again, this time heading for Knoxville, 185 winter miles away.

Several weeks later when Buck and I walked into Knoxville, the city was entangled in the worse winter storm in its history. We had gone south to avoid the bitter Midwest winters, yet on that day, temperatures plummeted and Knoxville made national news by vying with Akron, Ohio, for the role of coldest spot in the nation at minus 24 degrees. The city ground to a halt. Businesses of every kind locked their doors and closed up tight. The only movement on the streets was that of tow trucks rumbling over the icy roads, hauling jackknifed trucks from snow-filled ditches and rescuing stranded motorists whose cars were buried in the snow. Nobody else was out that day, not even a cat or a dog.

The following day, a most miserable Monday, Buck and I did not walk. But the next day we were out again. I added to my multiple layers a ski mask over my head and a chemically reacted heat pack pinned against my chest.

That day the land was frozen in silence. Our breath left our bodies and froze in the air, and for a while it looked as though the greatest threat to us would come from Buck himself, for sometimes when he ran to me he'd skid in tire tracks where snow had been pressed to ice. Too late he'd throw on the brakes, out of control. He couldn't stop in the ice-slick grooves and we'd both end up on the ground. Finally I scooped up a handful of snow, packed it into a ball, and threw it, smacking him on the rump, which of course he knew was play. He went chasing over the hills crazier than ever, flying over the powder, kicking it into the air, leaping up to catch it as it fell back to the ground.

On my left there was a gully, but Buck couldn't know that; snow had filled it in to road level. When Buck came back to play snowball again, he landed on the powder and fell into the trench. I cannot know what he fell upon, but what I can tell is this—whatever it was, it had to be sharp. When Buck climbed out of that gully, his foot was spouting blood. He limped a few steps then waited, looking to me for help.

I turned his paw and winced. His paw was cut right through a pad, deep inside his foot. The snow beneath his paw was stained a brilliant crimson red. I yanked the cord from my hood and laced it around his leg, with just enough tension to reduce the blood flow but not to cut it off. Still, Buck and I had a problem. It was midafternoon, which meant relief via Alex was hours away.

We had no choice. We had to keep moving. There was no question that if we had waited for help beside the road, we would have frozen to death. I kept Buck walking in the snow instead of on the road, hoping that the cold would help to congeal the blood. Every now and again we stopped to let him rest and I loosened the cord, then laced it again. Buck left red-stained pawprint tracks every step of the way.

It wasn't long before Buck's limp turned into a stumble. I gave him the last of the chocolate squares from my pocket, then, putting my hand through his collar, I lifted, not enough to choke him, but enough to relieve him of some of his weight. "You'll make it, Buck, you know you will. We've always made it before." But Buck was getting dull, and I was ready to carry my friend on my shoulders if I had to. Thank goodness Alex arrived before that was necessary, and we rushed Buck to a veterinarian.

The ugly cut in Buck's foot had to be closed and the vet gave us a choice. The most certain way for it to heal was to stitch it, but that would mean that Buck would have to stay off the foot for something like three weeks. Either he wouldn't walk with me or I'd have to wait for him. On the other hand, the vet said, we could pull the cut together by taping it closed. We could keep the wound clean by changing the tape each day. The advantage of using tape was that Buck could continue on the road. Alex and I decided it was worth a try. If it didn't work, we would come back to have the suturing done. We were too close now to the finish to contemplate Buck's missing out on the road. I just knew that if Buck could speak, he would have chosen the tape.

The vet showed us how to close the wound with a boot of tape. Every night I carefully removed it, bathed the cut, rubbed in some bag balm, and taped the wound up again. After a day or two of that, though, it was clear the cut wasn't healing. I figured that it could be because out on the road the bandage was getting wet. So I started wrapping the bandaged foot in many layers of plastic cut from supermarket bags. It didn't take Buck long to get used to a plastic-wrapped foot, but that didn't work, either. He soon wore through the plastic, and the bandage got wet again.

That evening I made a call to Guy. My son just happens to be one of those people who seem to be able to construct just about anything. Guy listened to Buck's problem, asked me to take a few measurements, including the length and width of his foot and the height of the leg up to the knee. Two days later an overnight express package arrived addressed to "Mr. Buck, Walking Across America." Inside the parcel were two handmade boots, exactly to Buck's size. One was made from corduroy, "for lounging," explained the note. The other was his "working boot." It was cut from an old pair of jeans, with the Calvin Klein label stitched across the front. They both had waterproof vinyl soles and three-inch zippers in the back, which closed them snug to his knee. After that Buck wore his working boot out on the road and the other one at night. It took only two weeks of wearing the boots before Buck's cut was beautifully healed.

Virginia signaled a turning point. From Oklahoma City on, we had been moving more or less straight across the South. In Bristol, on the Tennessee-Virginia border, we made that final tilt that turned us north and east. At long last, after fourteen months, we were zeroing in on the East.

Now we walked into spring. I saw snowdrifts thaw into the ground as ice that had formed on the banks of last year's streams grew porous, trickling drop by drop, in a search for newer paths. Meanwhile, slender blades of grass sprang from the sleeping soil. In Virginia the earth quickened its pulse and suddenly came awake.

But before that happened, while we were still in Bristol, my eagerness for spring nearly caused a disaster. For a few hours the sun broke through the clouds after months of gloomy skies. In my enthusiasm I threw open the camper's windows to let fresh air and sunlight in, then went out for a stroll with Buck to limber up my muscles. I came back to find Alex hunched over the computer and printer. He had the heater turned on high and aimed directly at the equipment. My enthusiasm for spring had misled me. The outside temperature was a mere minus 11 degrees and so of course was the air I'd let in. As a result, the mechanical parts of the printer were frozen and wouldn't move at all. It took Alex the better part of the morning to restore the printer to use.

We had roughly 370 miles to walk diagonally across Virginia, which would bring us into Washington, D.C., during the first week of April. We struck out for Roanoke, 140 miles away, while I kept my eyes open for more early signs of spring. Walking along a country road, we passed a weathered barn where I could see that last year's hay had been pitched inside. It wasn't stacked in tidy bales or in orderly jelly-roll forms, like many we had seen before. Nothing as modern as that. It was piled just the way I always thought hay should be stacked, in a great disheveled heap. Buck, with insatiable curiosity, ran into the barn. Quick as a flash he dashed back out, wrapped in spiderwebs and pursued by an indignant hen as mad as she could be. She shrieked and squawked and flew at him, jumped upon his back and beat him with her wings, and if Buck had a tail big enough to tuck beneath his legs, that's where it would have been.

"C'mon, Buck, leave her alone." But that little red hen wouldn't let up until she'd chased him back to the road. Only then she returned to her chicks and to scratching in the dirt. A few miles farther we walked to the peal of a church's carillon and I saw at the foot of a tree a crocus pushing through the snow.

Forty miles outside of Roanoke I stepped into a telephone booth to make a call I'd promised to make when we were back in Muskogee, Oklahoma. There we'd met Virginia and Wayne when they were traveling through on their way to California. They'd stopped at the table where we were planning our day's itinerary over a cup of coffee, to say some encouraging words, and ended with an invitation: "Now, if you get as far as Roanoke, you be sure to call. We'd like you to have dinner with us and the family." As they left, Virginia called out, as an afterthought, "Oh—what do you like to eat?"

"Pork chops" was the very first thing that had sprung to mind, "or anything at all—whatever the family likes."

So here we were, six months later, practically on their doorstep. "Hello, Virginia? This is the lady you invited to dinner back in Muskogee. Does it still stand?" There was a stunned silence on the other end of the line. It took Virginia several moments to recover; she had been certain that I wouldn't remember.

However, she quickly rounded up the family and three nights later we had a wonderful time filled with laughter when Virginia, Wayne, Alex and I, their daughters and husbands, and grandchildren, crowded around the dining room table, in the middle of which sat the whoppingest stack of pork chops I had ever seen.

It was just north of Roanoke that Buck and I walked the Blue Ridge and crossed the Appalachian Trail. I knew that once we entered Washington, D.C., it would be some time before we would walk through rolling hills and tangled brush in crisp clean mountain air. So I basked in the placid pleasures of the Blue Ridge hills and tried to outdo the wind by flurrying up mountains of rusty leaves, stirring them up with my feet.

A few days later Buck and I passed a unique geological bridge formation called Natural Bridge, and just beyond it we came to a private zoo, where the owner, in work jeans and red flannel shirt, was cleaning up the grounds. Karl's round face had the healthy glow that comes from working outdoors and the kindly appearance of one who understands and loves animals. Buck and I stopped to say hello and it wasn't long before Karl invited us inside. I hesitated because of Buck, but Karl, with an instinct for animals, had already assessed him. Nevertheless, I clipped him onto his leash before we stepped inside the zoo.

To my delight, many of the animals were not in cages, so we walked among such petable animals as curious llamas and strutting peacocks with tails spread into fans. I noticed that the more timid ostriches pulled away from us. Buck was, quite naturally, extraordinarily curious about the exotic animals, and I'm sure he would have loved to run among them, sniffing at the cages of tropical birds and monkeys sitting beneath the petting zoo's candy-striped roofs.

Soon we were approaching one cage a short distance away when Buck froze in his tracks. His eyes nearly fell from his head. He dug in his heels and refused to budge when he saw the tigers. I patted his shoulder to reassure him. "It's all right, Buck," I soothed, but Buck was unwilling to be convinced. He lay right down on the ground and balked against his leash, stubbornly refusing to move even an inch. "Buck," I reasoned with him, "it really is okay." But he adamantly declined to believe me. I continued to urge him on, and with great reluctance he obliged, although most begrudgingly, and dropped into a crouch, ready to spring if needed.

These tigers watched us approaching, slowing their nervous

tread momentarily to look at us, then quickening their restless pace. Then they growled. Buck's eyes were glued on the tigers, and although I'd never seen him show fear before, there was no doubt that Buck was downright afraid. His flanks were out of control, shaking and trembling wildly while he crept, though most unwillingly, closer to the cage.

An outer fence, about four feet high, surrounded the tigers' cage. Karl swung open a gate and, raising his brows in a question, inquired, "Want to come in here?"

It was late in the afternoon and shadows were cast to the east when Alex returned and found us there. "Some interesting pictures can be taken here," he said, removing the camera from its cover.

Since the last rays of sun were shining on the farthest side of the cage, we'd have to stand there in order to get good pictures. I placed Buck on my left, the side farthest from the cage, and led him around the enclosure to the opposite side of the cage, where he stood just behind me and a little to my left. Alex placed the lens of the camera through the wire fence and then, to steady his grip, leaned against the cage, focusing on a tiger crouched behind a stump. The tiger kept his yellow eyes steadily on Alex as though sizing up his prey; just the tip of his tail was moving, twitching up and down.

Then, just as Alex clicked the shutter, the tiger made his play. With nails extended and a bloodcurdling roar, he sprang from behind the log and crashed upon the fence, knocking Alex backward. The film caught the tiger vaulting through the air. It had happened much too fast for Alex or me to react, although apparently not for Buck. With animal instinct he'd seen the attack coming and tore loose from his leash. He soared right over my shoulder, crashing on the cage. The animals met on the wire, snarling ferociously, as Buck held on with his teeth. He hung like that until I steadied myself to pull him loose from the fence.

Now when people say to me, as sometimes they have done, that they think that I am courageous for having taken this walk, I'm quick to tell them about Buck, who showed me what courage is. On that day I saw courage in action when Buck surmounted his fear and came to Alex's defense to fight against a tiger, even though he must have realized that he didn't stand a chance.

Just a stone's throw from Washington, D.C., we walked through a landscape as rural as those we'd found in Arkansas and Tennessee. It was the crush of traffic that let me know more clearly than anything else that we were approaching the Capital. At 2:30 in the afternoon a steady stream of traffic flowed by and I noticed that the traffic noise in my right ear was dim. I put my finger into it and shook. "I'll have it looked at," I promised myself, thinking it might be the only permanent casualty from my journey.

We passed a simple one-room structure, propped up on cinder blocks. A hand-lettered sign read "The Headquarters of the Holy Spirit." The landscape was pastoral all right, yet overhead a Concorde screamed through the sky heading into Dulles Airport.

Buck and I entered Washington by crossing the Potomac River and then headed down Canal Road following the river-bank. We turned into Georgetown where before an apartment building a green-uniformed doorman with gleaming epaulets and braid caught an eyeful of Buck and jumped back from the curb. "Man, sure hope your dog's had breakfast," he exclaimed, taking refuge inside the lobby. There was a produce truck backed up to a curb, its scale swung from a chain. There seemed to be something appealing about buying veggies from the back of a produce truck in towns of every size. The produce man was doing a stiff business and no one seemed to notice that the crates of eggs sitting in the sun on the sidewalk had a supermarket stamp on their side.

A little farther we came to a storefront fortune-teller. Now, I had seen them in towns of every size all across the land, but here, where decisions of worldwide importance are made? I couldn't resist seeking her counsel. I left Buck outside (his palm would be too difficult to read anyway!) and entered the room where others were waiting their turn. I wiped my palms on my knees. Maybe, I thought, she'd tell me something that I might not want to hear, but I stayed anyway.

Madame Marie came through a curtain and beckoned me with her finger into a simple room with two chairs and a table upon which really sat the proverbial crystal ball. She didn't look like a gypsy at all, dressed as she was in a gray tweed suit instead of a peasant dress, but I'd come this far, so while Buck watched through the window, she turned my hand and studied the lines on my palm. For fifteen dollars she told me, "You've come a long way." How did she know? Peering at me intently: "Hummm—and I see you are going much farther." That wasn't so bad. "Your marriage?" She tilted her head and frowned. What does that mean? I wondered. "Yes, it is a good one. Right here, see"—she pointed with a tapered nail to a line on my palm—"it will last a long time." Well, nothing wrong about that. For twenty-five dollars more I could have a complete reading, but I figured I'd heard enough. Before I left, I couldn't help but mutter: "This is where those who guide my fate come for answers? The Pentagon is guided by Tarot?"

She smiled and leaned forward to whisper, in a confidential tone, "Yes—they are the ones who come."

It was Easter week and the cherry blossoms were in full bloom. The Capital was teeming with tourists, including thousands of high school seniors who had come from all over the country, eager to see their government at work. The unceasing sounds of the city clamored in my ears, buses grinding gears, taxies honking as they ran lights, vendors hawking T-shirts—the city ruckus carried late into the humid night and I began to feel a pervading weariness press down on me that I hadn't felt when I was out on the road.

We wound our way along M Street, then south on Seventeenth, to keep a commitment to all the young people who had asked me, "Are you going to visit the White House?" And I'd promised that I would. So for just that reason Buck and I stood for a few moments in the Ellipse, across from the White House, at the Zero Milestone marker, the stone from which all distances in the United States are computed, including the ones we'd walked.

Once I'd been a city girl but it seemed as though that was a thing of the past. I was getting jumpy, although we stayed in Washington long enough to respect the eighteen speaking engagements to which I had committed myself. But the day we were set to get back on the road, I was more than ready.

We took Seventeenth Street out of town, I made a short stop at the zoo, and farther on I stopped again to enter a Zen meditation center. I sat there for a while to still myself again. I needed the quiet. From here on, to the end of the journey, Buck and I would face big cities, one after another, and roads snarled with traffic. I was no longer used to them.

By the time we had arrived in D.C., I had actually thought that nothing would ever seem difficult again. Now I knew that the remaining miles *would* be difficult—differently so from most of our previous journey. In the next 140 miles, a distance that to Buck and me was a snap of the fingers now, we would walk through Baltimore and Philadelphia and then head toward New York City. For months on end, Buck and I for the most part had been sheltered from big-city clatter. When we walked these metropolitan areas, I saw more than ever the inner-city decay surrounding islands of speciality shops, the newspaper stands chained to lampposts, trash bins overflowing, and billboards sprayed with paint. I walked shoulder to shoulder in city congestion and was elbowed off curbs. I had a new insight into why those who are wedged so close together create greater personal distance, how this makes them develop an outer crust of indifference. Why, I even understand their need for Walkman radios clamped to their ears. It seems the closer people crowd, the greater their isolation.

What about those, I got to thinking, who have isolation even greater than that, those whose actions for whatever reasons have confined them behind bars? Underneath these crusts we have created, do we all feel just the same? In Philadelphia I went to the House of Correction.

I was taken to the facilities in an official prison vehicle. I tried to imagine what it could be like to be riding in that automobile involuntarily. I couldn't, not really. After we pulled into the sprawling dreary yard and went into the building, where heavy iron gates were unlocked and slammed shut behind me one after another with resounding vibrations, my skin ran cold. In those dim, drab corridors I began to get a sense of the futile, ominous permanence that I might feel from being sealed in there.

"This will be your toughest audience," I was told.

"Why do you say that?"

"They don't much care for heroines. Besides, you will be competing for their attention—this is their break time. They have a chance to buy candy and things they really like. But they might come straggling in."

A section of a room had been set up with chairs, two of which were occupied. I could hear others laughing in the corridor. With an audience of two, I began. Abruptly one of the women stood up and left. I still had an audience of one, and I wasn't going to let her down. But the woman who had left the room surprised me when she came back with several others, and slowly the seats began to fill with the curious and those with scoffing faces. Soon a broad-faced woman, sitting center front, leaned back in her chair.

"All right, sister, just why did you do it?" she demanded, while others peeled candy bars and shared potato chips.

Sure, I thought to myself, why would they want to hear about America when they might never see it? Still, I started my tale from the Pacific Coast and wound across the country, telling them quite simply about the wonders of the land and the beauty of its people, even though it seemed incongruous to be speaking thus to them, some of whom had never been beyond their neighborhood and maybe never would. After a while I noticed that the candy rested on their laps, and that there was silence.

We had been given a very short time in which to have a visit and all too soon that time was up. As I prepared to leave, a voice spoke from the rear.

"Now that you seen it, what do you think—I mean is there any hope?"

I didn't need to answer. I heard a thoughtful muted voice come from the back: "There's always hope. It's up to us to keep it alive. Then when we get out of here, to pass it on to others."

Could it be said any better?

That day I left carrying with me little scraps of paper on which they had scribbled their wishes, which turned out to be for things like "I pray my children is safe until I get back" and "I don't want my kids to do nothing what I did cause I know it's wrong—and it's terrible to be in here." Some wrote messages for a world of peace.

What I learned from the House of Correction is that underneath it all, we all want the same of life. I tucked their paper wishes into my pocket along with the penny that had been riding there for so many months and promised that at the ocean I would set them free.

I was early. I had more than enough time to keep the commitment I'd made to be at the Statue of Liberty on the Fourth of July 1985. It had been planned that way. Now no unexpected event could keep me from that day. We knew that our first plan, which was to be on Liberty Island on that day, had to be changed. The island was now closed to visitors while

Lady Liberty underwent restoration, but wrapped in scaffolding or not, she would look beautiful to me. We would end the journey as close as possible, which would be at Liberty State Park.

The extra time gave me a chance to walk down to Atlantic City, where I could complete the ocean-to-ocean part of my journey, and throw the penny in my pocket into the Atlantic Ocean instead of the Hudson River.

I now had a jar full of pennies. I had found them scattered everywhere across America, some in the most unlikely spots, places so remote that I wondered how it could possibly be that another person had been there, too. I found the first one early in the journey, when Buck and I were on our way to Death Valley. I had gone way back into a cluster of desert yucca to find a convenience station of the road, looking for privacy farther back than I would later find necessary, and took refuge under a tall, way-over-my-head yucca plant. The leaf of the yucca is slender, ending in a spike. The lower leaves are dry and droopy, pointing toward the ground, and when I tried to move away I was pinned in place, the spikes impaling my skin. To make matters even worse, red ants had climbed up onto my shoes and were moving toward my legs. I couldn't stand and I could stay, so I fell onto my belly and crawled through the sand until I was free of the spines. I got back on my feet and was brushing ants and sand from my clothes when I spotted, of all things, a penny on the ground. Now, how could I leave this penny behind? So I dropped it into my pocket where it jingled with the other one until I was back at the camper, and that's when I began my collection.

On Friday, June 7, we were in Atlantic City on the boardwalk where students from Atlantic City's junior high school, Mayor Usry, and I cast our wishes for a harmonious world, sending them out to sea. I waded into the ocean and kept my promise to the reporter back in California by throwing his penny as far as I could and making a wish for world peace. The now shiny penny shimmered in the sun before it dropped into the ocean and its ripples began their journey, while the paper wishes from Philadelphia were scattered over the water and carried on the wind.

The same buffer of time that had allowed the journey to Atlantic City also made it possible to accept the invitation we'd received to return to Baltimore to participate in the National Flag Day ceremonies. But before we left I decided to see about my right ear. It seemed I had gone deaf. I heard absolutely nothing with it. But if that was the price to pay for the journey, so be it.

"How long have you had the problem?" the physician asked while probing with the otoscope into the left ear—I had no trouble with that one.

"Several months. It's been getting worse progressively."

"Don't see anything wrong in there," he said. "Let's take a look at the other." He peered around inside the right one. "Hmmmm, now, that's strange," he said; I sure didn't like the sound of that. Maybe it was worse than I thought. He stepped back and eyed me strangely. "What kind of work do you do?"

Why in the world would he ask that? I thought. I told him what I'd been up to for the past year and a half. I saw an expression of amusement cross his face.

"Which side of the road do you walk on?" he asked.

"The left. Why?"

"So the right ear faces the traffic?"

"Yes."

And now he was laughing. "I don't know just how to tell you this, but there is absolutely nothing wrong with your ear. Other than it is without a doubt the dirtiest ear I have ever seen."

Well, under any other circumstances that might be embarrassing, but we had a good laugh over it.

When I left, my ear was singing again, having been swept clean of deeply embedded desert sand, auto exhaust, maybe a little pollen—in other words, a seventeen-month collection of roadside dust and grit.

On June 14 we were back in Baltimore, sitting within the protection of Fort McHenry's small courtyard, waiting with other guests for the ceremonies to begin. Each guest held a small American flag while larger ones fluttered loosely on the parapets, gracefully waving against a cloudless sky. The crowd's murmurs were politely restrained; still, there was an unmistakable undercurrent of heartfelt patriotism that energized the air.

Suddenly a giant helicopter descended from the sky, its whirling blades creating such a stir that it caused the flags to billow. It settled on the grass outside the courtyard walls. Only minutes later we rose to honor the President and Mrs. Reagan as they strode through the gates. It was impossible not to be touched by the unity of spirit in that courtyard. There wasn't a heartbeat there that wasn't roused when we heard the strains of "The Star-Spangled Banner" wafting through the air, and our hands went over our hearts and we turned to salute our flag.

We were back in New Jersey on June 21 with 100 miles and fourteen days to complete the journey. I was on my eighteenth pair of shoes. For the most part we followed Highway 9, taking occasional diversions by striking out into the woods. The woods of New Jersey are deep, dark, and sometimes impenetrable. The sandy trails that wind in and out between the trees seem to lead everywhere and nowhere, and I suspect that by following them one can get lost in the Pinelands forever. I remember reading once that the living organisms on a body at any one time exceed the human population of the world, and in New Jersey it looked like Buck had got them all. The mysterious system of waterways that trickles through the woods breeds mosquitoes, green head flies, and ticks, and Buck had every one. But it didn't slow him down at all.

Where the trees have been cleared, corn ripens in a patchwork of small farms, while just across the road from the cornstalks, peppers and tomatoes hang on the vines. I stopped at produce stands along the way and was skeptical when told that New Jersey produce is the best in the world, "Better than California's." But I have to admit there's something to it—maybe it's the iron-rich soil. Whatever the reason, New Jersey produce has robust flavor. Why, when you bite into a tomato, it leaps into your mouth.

Only 40 miles from our destination, we walked roads where cattails, those tall reedy plants with furry spikes, grow naturally in the marsh, and I thought back upon how delighted I'd been every time I'd seen a familiar plant in its natural setting: wild marigolds along the coast, flowering cactus in the desert, iris in the mountains, paper-whites springing up from nowhere, rhododendrons in the forests of the East. With one week to go I knew Buck and I would reach our goal and I was happy . . . I was sad. I couldn't believe it was almost over.

CONCLUSION

When a Dream Is Fulfilled

Walking across the country has been a little like walking across my life, although in faster motion. Now those eighteen months and 3,900 miles with two feet on the ground were nearly over. The trip had not been easy, but when I began the walk, I'd known it wouldn't be, and, anyway, challenge is the stuff from which growth is most likely to sprout. Besides, wherever is it written that difficult should ever mean not going for our dreams?

But what can you do with a dream fulfilled? I'd already thought it over. Share it, and then create another, because dreams, like love, get dusty when they're not renewed.

I'm the kind of person who kicks nails off the road and I rather like the feeling that comes from knowing there are fewer flat tires out there as a result of Buck and me traveling down some of those paths. I also like to think that if with every step we left behind a world that's a little better, perhaps we helped, if only a little, to pull the world together.

America is its people, and when you get to talking with them, you discover that there are many more Americans out there doing things right than the other way around.

On the Fourth of July 1985, at 10:00 A.M., Buck and I completed the last mile. Buck was dressed up for the occasion. I had changed his surveyor's-tape ribbons for more appropriate red, white, and blue ones. We walked along Statue of Liberty Drive, an avenue of fluttering flags, accompanied by Jersey City Mayor Cucci and my sons, Gary and Guy, who flew in to join us on that very special day. The night before, Alex and I had spoken our thoughts of joy to each other, and he was now taking pictures for our memories.

We walked to the end of Liberty State Park when tears suddenly broke loose, streaming down my cheeks as though a dam had burst. I couldn't hold them back. There she stood across the bay just as I remembered, Miss Liberty, a symbol for freedom as much today as when she'd come to these shores so many years ago, an immigrant herself.

We were not alone in the shadow of Lady Liberty. A happy friendly crowd had cheered the last mile and someone turned to ask me. "What are you going to do when you get back home?"

"Create another dream," I said, knowing that home for me now meant everyplace.

Two men in dark, three-piece business suits were standing beside me, and because I had been mulling the question around myself for a while, I casually turned and asked them, "How would you define freedom?"

"I think," one said after reflection, "it's the right to make choices."

And the other replied, "Yes, I think it's the freedom to make choices that do not injure others."

I saw a youngster of about eight years of age balancing on the rocks at the water's edge. He had been listening. "I think I know," he said, looking up shyly and squinting against the sun. "It means . . . beautiful."

CHRISTIAN HERALD
People Making A Difference

Christian Herald is a family of dedicated, Christ-centered ministries that reaches out to deprived children in need, and to homeless men who are lost in alcoholism and drug addiction. Christian Herald also offers the finest in family and evangelical literature through its book clubs and publishes a popular, dynamic magazine for today's Christians.

Our Ministries

Family Bookshelf and **Christian Bookshelf** provide a wide selection of inspirational reading and Christian literature written by best-selling authors. All books are recommended by an Advisory Board of distinguished writers and editors.

Christian Herald magazine is contemporary, a dynamic publication that addresses the vital concerns of today's Christian. Each monthly issue contains a sharing of true personal stories written by people who have found in Christ the strength to make a difference in the world around them.

Christian Herald Children. The door of God's grace opens wide to give impoverished youngsters a breath of fresh air, away from the evils of the streets. Every summer, hundreds of youngsters are welcomed at the Christian Herald Mont Lawn Camp located in the Poconos at Bushkill, Pennsylvania. Year-round assistance is also provided, including teen programs, tutoring in reading and writing, family counseling, career guidance and college scholarship programs.

The Bowery Mission. Located in New York City, the Bowery Mission offers hope and Gospel strength to the downtrodden and homeless. Here, the men of Skid Row are fed, clothed, ministered to. Many voluntarily enter a 6-month discipleship program of spiritual guidance, nutrition therapy and Bible study.

Our Father's House. Located in rural Pennsylvania, Our Father's House is a discipleship and job training center. Alcoholics and drug addicts are given an opportunity to recover, away from the temptations of city streets.

Christian Herald ministries, founded in 1878, are supported by the voluntary contributions of individuals and by legacies and bequests. Contributions are tax deductible. Checks should be made out to Christian Herald Children, The Bowery Mission, or to Christian Herald Association.

Administrative Office: 40 Overlook Drive, Chappaqua, New York 10514
Telephone: (914) 769-9000

 Fully-accredited Member of the Evangelical Council for Financial Accountability